AROUND THE SOUND

AMUSING THOUGHTS AND TALES FROM WASHINGTON'S PUGET SOUND

BY

JOSH KILEN

Cantonfield Media
2367 Tacoma Aveenue South
Tacoma, WA 98402
253-353-2011
www.cantonfield.com

Ordering Information:
Quantity sales. Special discounts are available on quantity purchases by corporations, associations, and others. For details, contact the publisher at the address above.

Printed in the United States of America

First Printing, 2016

ISBN 978-1532777769

DEDICATION

To Megan,

For encouraging my silly and always encouraging
me no matter what.

More Titles from Josh Kilen

The Tales of Big and Little
Doom of the Three Stones
Shirlee's Revenge
The End of the Worlds

The Lost Princess Series
The Lost Princess in Winter's Grip
The Lost Princess in The Shifting Sands
The Lost Princess in Destiny's Call

The Adventures of Sean Ryanis
Sean Ryanis & The Impossible Chase
Sean Ryanis & The Brink of Oblivion

The Superhero Chronicles
Birth of Moonlight

Just a Little Apocalypse

Non-Fiction Titles
Walking the Narrow Road: Instruction for Christians In Business
Social Joy: Marketing for Artists
Choreawseome!
Go Write Now
Killer Deals
Electing to Win

TABLE OF CONTENTS

INTRODUCTION

I hope that you read this in the bathroom.

I know that that's an odd request, but I really think my material plays best in rooms of reprieve. The acoustics will be more supportive of your laughter (think about how amazing your laughs will sound echoing off the bathroom walls), but also, this book doesn't lend itself to long, intense study. It's a short read, filled with odd but funny stories.

Over the years, I've written pieces about local towns I visited in the Pacific Northwest's Puget Sound area, short essays on various subjects like my Dad wearing speedos or the Taliban's bureaucracy problems (and solutions!), and all with an eye to make people chuckle to themselves in a way that makes strangers worry about their sanity. I hope that I succeeded, but the hard part was figuring out how to combine all of these different stories into one book.

Thankfully, that dilemma was resolved by my intense laziness. 'Just put them all into one book' my lazy self said. 'What's going on here?' my small, hard-working self said, but he was drowned and shot twice by the lazy one in a rare fit of action. Thus, this book.

Whether you read this in the bathroom, on a subway, or in your favorite comfy chair, I hope you enjoy these amusing stories from my home.

TOWNS AROUND THE SOUND

POULSBO, WA

In my experience, most retail employees are mildly unhelpful at best and excrete a firm belief that life is nothing if not a lack of opportunities. So it was a revelation when an earnestly cheerful middle-aged woman working at the donut shop in downtown Poulsbo implored me to move to her town. This wonderful donut woman, Diane, managed to warm the room with just her smile and pleasant demeanor. She even gave me a free cookie, then put her finger in front of her lips, "shushing" me like it was our little secret. I was immediately charmed, but that seems to be the way things go in this sleepy coastal town.

Poulsbo began as a small fishing village on the Kitsap peninsula, a safe haven for immigrants from Norway and Finland. Though some Swedes were allowed to live on the fringes of town, the original inhabitants tried to keep the population free from the "evils" of Swedish influence. Norwegian and Swedish peoples, at least in the Americas, continue this enthusiastic and long-standing feud. Today, the battle is waged through joke books and coffee mugs disparaging the other side's inferiorities, such as "Norwegians are dumb and lazy" or "Swedes are crafty and treacherous." The battle must be great, or at least great enough to keep the shops that sell this type of swag in business.

The Norwegians chose the Poulsbo area because it reminded them a good deal of Norway. The deep harbors, plentiful woods, abundant wildlife, the moderately unpleasant but endurable climate all hearkened back to the place that they had just mightily struggled to leave. The original settlers wrote home about the beauty of the area, and they weren't wrong--it's a striking bay with views of snowcapped mountains and rolling waves gently splashing against the many docks. But its beauty is only actively visible on a warm, sunny day, which in Washington State happens on average two weeks out of the year. Norwegians, never wanting too much of a good thing, as a rule, found this refreshing I'm sure.

In fact, it's a very Norwegian trait to find something just slightly better than where they came from, and no more. My own great, great grandfather Carl left the family farm which was nestled in a quintessential Norwegian valley, close to a small, dreary stream, for the wild promise of life in the United States. He promptly moved to Minnesota to build a small farm in a valley, next to a plain river. Minnesota had an extra week of warmth, which was all the adventure Carl required. Norwegians are a simple people in this respect. Carl's descendants migrated ever farther west, moving to North Dakota, and eventually to Washington. I imagine that when they found their way to Washington State, it must have seemed a bit like Valhalla.

The city's name was a mistake. It stemmed from a careless clerical error, breathtakingly common in those days. The tale begins with the second family to found Poulsbo, headed by Ivar B. Moe, who, after several years of watching the local population grow, decided to petition on the town's behalf for a post office in 1886. Having your own post office was quite a big deal in those days, a sign that your small town was worthy of governmental notice. Not only that, but the official language of the town was Norwegian (an ordinance that would not be remedied until after World War II). A local postmaster who spoke the language would help the many families sending letters back to Norway, presumably to regale them with tales of Poulsbo's similarities to the native land.

Since the community at that time had no official name, Moe petitioned that the name be established as Paulsbo, or literally "Paul's Place", named after a small fishing village in Norway where Moe spent his formative years. The petition was granted and Moe was made the first Postmaster, though the intended name of the town never saw the light of day. The

Postmaster General in Washington DC, hard of sight and harried by his many duties, had a difficult time reading Moe's handwriting. The "a," looking too much like an "o," was changed, despite the grammatical anomaly. I'm sure the Postmaster was inundated with spellings that seemed all too foreign, so rather than stop and think about the name, he scribbled it down as Poulsbo, and the name has stuck ever since. Norwegians generally don't like to make a fuss.

Poulsbo has some rather distinct zones of habitation, the first being the vast and unsettling commercialization along the main highway running through the town. Popping up on the side of the road, every imaginable retail convenience storms into view, from fast food restaurants to mega home improvement centers. They even have a mammoth Walmart, the kind that sells everything you could possibly want at prices that ensure you will come back for replacements in a year's time. It's a very sad truth that most casual drivers merely take the highway through the town and mistakenly assume this to be the extent of Poulsbo's charms. And who could blame them--the over-commercialization of small towns is a rather common sight these days.

As the population of a town expands, more services are required to maintain its livability. As more people discover the tranquil wonder of the small town, the population grows. When populations spike, large businesses try to hone in on the action. Soon, instead of the local burger joint, there's a Burger King. Instead of Moe's Grocery, you have Safeway. People eventually appreciate the convenience that these larger chain establishments bring, but none of them can embody the spirit of the small town. Out of necessity, the town changes a bit, and not for the better. Chains are simply too common and universally boring. If you see one Safeway or Walmart, chances are you would not find yourself shocked into silent admiration when you step into another one 2000 miles away. So, as with any small town that has the propensity to build up a rather gaudy commercial district, to really see Poulsbo you have to get off the main road.

Moving away from the commercialism for a moment, one of Poulsbo's finest features is its older residential neighborhood, located on the main hill overlooking the picturesque bay. Drive down the gently winding streets and you will notice they are pleasantly wide and free from rubbish, stained couches with "FREE" signs on them, or anything that might spoil the local beauty. Whether they employ nimble-fingered elves or simply have a community overly dedicated to the abolishment of detritus from their streets, the town looks marvelously settled and happy. Many houses are turn-of-the-century Victorians and craftsmen, all phenomenally maintained and worthy of a long, slow, perhaps slightly creepy drive (if viewed through more suspicious eyes) past their immaculate lawns. White picket fences line the sidewalks, giving the whole place an air of small town prosperity rarely seen these days. And there is not a chain link fence to be seen, except at the expansive public recreational park, where such things should be reasonably allowed.

The perfection of the town begins to pull you in and before you know it, you can't help but entertain the impossible idea of moving there that day. Poulsbo looks like a wonderful place to raise your kids, the kind of place where you live on a beautifully apportioned cul-de-sac, every one of our neighbors would be cheerful and caring, and your days would know a quality of happiness not seen since the 1950s. Your kids would grow up to be the talk of the town, you and your spouse would be pillars of the community, and life would be marvelous.

All these thoughts and more filled my head on one of my casual jaunts with the family into Poulsbo. As we drove around the neighborhoods I imagined us living there. I even began to quietly hum, much to my wife's amusement. We casually looked for available property and noticed a decided lack of "For

Sale" signs which was at once encouraging and disappointing. On the one hand, this town was desirable enough that people wanted to stay (plus Norwegians are known for their fiscal frugality, so you won't catch them in any high-risk mortgages, eventually forced to abandon their homes). But the pickings were slim. After a brief tour up and down a few streets, my wife asked me to stop in front of what I can only describe as a monument to American opulence.

Occasionally my wife and I play this game where we pretend we can afford things like million dollar houses. It's a fun game until I start to do the math, which introduces the ugly element of reality that spoils everything. I was instructed to grab a flyer, "just for fun." I ran up to the For Sale sign and took one of the handy fact sheets to bring back for everyone in the car. I hid the price from myself on purpose, knowing that my wife preferred me not to know, thereby ruining the imaginative exercise.

I saw it on accident. Walking back to the car, my brain engaged in a grand form of mathematical gymnastics. The stress of amortization formulas must have showed heavy on my face. At least, I assume so, since the first thing my wife said was, "You looked, didn't you?" It wasn't really a question and I assumed the guilt on my face was the only answer she needed.

"I honestly tried not to," which was true. She

sighed with the resignation that comes naturally to anyone who lives with me, "Okay, how much is it?"

I showed her the flyer, "$799,000! Can you believe it?" I was sure she would see the absurdity of it all.

To my surprise, she looked thoughtful, "That's not bad," she said with a casual air as if we were discussing the price of a cup of coffee or light bulbs.

"Not bad! Are you serious? I know it's 6 bedrooms, 4 and ¾ bath, has a library, a pool, beautiful Victorian features combined with modern conveniences and generally takes one's breath away to look at, but really, that's $4500 a month in mortgage payments. A bit much don't you think?"

She slowly shook her head, "Not really, we could make it work." I couldn't tell if she was trying to rile me up or not, but the blood boiled anyway.

"I could think of so many things we could spend that money on besides..." That's when I looked at her face and saw the profound disappointment she was going feel if I continued down my thrifty line of reasoning. I changed directions with a sigh, "I guess I'll have to sell more books."

"That's the spirit," she smiled and patted my leg.

A note to the reader which, if you are male, may help in your future female relations. My wife is not materialistic, and I doubt yours is either. She might spend a small fortune on art supplies or birthday presents, but she would never pressure me to just make money to buy bigger and better things. What she does want is the possibility (read: fantasy) of having these things, which to her is just about as good as having them. For this, I'm perpetually thankful.

What she doesn't want is for me to crap all over her fantasy. There's no other way to put it. My advice to all males: don't dump on your woman's materialistic fantasies, ever. Chances are, they're just that--fantasy--and she's quite content with whatever level of wealth that you currently provide. Otherwise, she wouldn't likely spend more time with you than is absolutely necessary. Of course, if you happened to surprise her one sunny day with a $800k Victorian mansion in Poulsbo, I'm sure she wouldn't be too upset about the act of spontaneous generosity.

Once you have taken in your fill of the fine residential district, it's time to meander to the downtown waterfront. Without a doubt, it is one of the finer small town main streets Washington State has to offer. Ignoring the retail empire of the highway, Poulsbo has managed to contain its smaller commercial endeavors along Front Street, which stretches for only a mile or so along the waterfront. It's the kind of place where every shop manages to look eternally welcoming and busy. Tourists and locals alike wander up and down the sidewalks in that slow gait that shoppers get when they are taking it all in and making a day out of commercial behavior.

Small town shopping is commercialization at its best. Never once have I had the same feeling being greeted when I walk into a Walmart as I do when I'm greeted walking into a local small business. There's a wonderful earnestness about the small business that makes me feel like they need me; like my purchase could keep them afloat, at least for one more day.

The flip side of that is that I feel like a heel when I'm just looking around and don't intend to purchase anything, but I like to know that if I did, it would mean quite a lot. I never get that same feeling of importance at a larger retailer. Maybe it's the consistent failure of the greeter to look moderately interested in their one and only job--greeting--or the oppressively mammoth size of the building. Or perhaps it's the hive of bodies entering and exiting constantly that make me question my worth to the corporation. In any case, I prefer to deal with local whenever possible, unless I need something cheap, or at off hours, or the mega store is closer. Shut up, I shop local when I can.

When you drive down into the thriving downtown area, beginning when Hostmark Street turns into Front Street and continuing for at least a half mile, you'll notice immediately a sense of happiness around the whole town, as if any unpleasantness is not tolerated within this square mile of shops. Each shop looks as if it wanted to be there, and a quick peek inside reveals shopkeepers excited to see you and, of course, your wallet. But never once do you get the feeling that you're required to buy anything, just that they are happy to have you around. This makes going into each shop an adventure as opposed to a burden.

Walking down Poulsbo's main street and patronizing its many fine shops made me realize that that's how I feel at places like the mall, an enormous burden to everyone. Every person and every item are the same at the mall and no one cares about either. It's all the same stuff, the same looks, the same people. In this town, however, everything has character and your business matters. I love it.

Which leads me to the wonderful woman who wanted me to move to Poulsbo.

Sluys Poulsbo Bakery is a must see destination in Poulsbo. In addition to large, fluffy, flavorful donuts they offer traditional Norwegian and Scandinavian pastries, fresh baked bread, and lots of small town character. You would think that such crowds would present a rather weighty difficulty for the mostly young folks behind the donut counter--who all look as if High School were an ambition--but they managed the crowd with a grace that belied their ages. You step in line, order some confections, and are expertly swept along to pick up your goods and pay. It looks like madness but works like clockwork. As I paid, I mentioned to Diane that this was my first foray into the small but wonderful world of Poulsbo. She asked where I was coming from, and I told her Port Orchard. She shook her head in sympathy and that's when she enjoined me to relocate. I told her that I would give it some serious thought and left to enjoy the pastries.

There are many fine shops in addition to Sluys and one of them sells chocolates, much to my wife's joy. Boehm's Chocolates is a confectionery with heart. The store is charming and spacious, and located beneath the giant Viking mural, which is wonderful. The quality of the candies that they produce is worth a trip alone and the prices are quite reasonable, which makes my thrifty heart happier than I can say. One oddity about the store, while the chocolates and candy are first rate, is that the rest of the merchandise is the type of gift shop swag that belongs in the attic of your craziest aunt. You know, the one with more cats than sense. Enjoy the divine chocolate, but leave the porcelain milk maids on the shelf.

In a building slightly up the hill from Boehm's is

a store called Marina Market which looks exactly like an old Qwiki-Mart of the "they can't have anything interesting in there because it's a Quiki-Mart" variety, but once you step inside, you realize the immensity of your mistake. Marina's is the coolest convenience store in all of God's wondrous creation. Fitting perfectly in the Euro tradition of the town, Marina's is not your typical Qwiki-Mart. Instead of the usual bland wares, you would see in any Am-Pm or 7-11, they have hand-selected the most interesting assortment of goods, from custom spices to hundreds of craft beers, and even a wide variety of canned meats. I have no idea how they pack so much into such a small space, but I often find myself pleasantly occupied for at least an entire hour reading the labels on European cookie packages, sorting through the pickled herrings, and drooling over the lovely selection of adult beverages. One in particular caught my eye, called Viking's Blood, and I was very keen to try it. But at $32 a bottle, I was less than willing to pay the exorbitant cost, and left it to my imagination.

Across the street is perhaps the most lovingly appointed bookstore in existence. Liberty Bay Books, named for the scenic body of water outside its door, is not a large bookstore by any stretch of the imagination, but they use the space in such creative and intriguing ways that you feel as if you could browse there for hours. In fact, that's what many do.

It's safe to say that my family loves a good bookstore. We have spent many happy hours looking for our favorite genres, comparing notes, and generally giving in to our more nerd-like tendencies. As I browsed the quality selection of travel and how-to books, the proprietor must have asked me if I needed anything three or four times. Normally I would find this behavior off-putting and generally disagreeable, but she was able to ask in ways just different enough to be engaging. I found a book I had been searching for for the past two months, purchased it, and left with a hearty smile on my face.

Next door is a coffee shop that should serve as the standard for all other coffee/deli operations. When you walk into Hot Shots Java, you are instantly hit with a deep sense of contentment, like this is where you should always drink your coffee, eat a bagel, and talk with your neighbor about the plumbing. It simply feels like a coffee shop should feel. I walked up to the counter, grinning that small smile you get when you are unreasonably happy. Bethany, the barista, took my order (always black coffee) and filled it right away. When she handed me my sweet dark nectar, I noticed a piece of chocolate in the divot on the lid of my cup. I asked about that and Bethany informed me that they get their coffee bean chocolates from Bohemes and like to include them in everyone's drinks. Of course they do, I thought. One sip of the coffee and I knew that no cream or sweetener was needed; it was delightful. I reluctantly left Hot Shots with its fun, homey energy. There was probably a small skip in my step.

It's worth noting that Starbucks exists in Upper Poulsbo in the largely commercial area, but not in the downtown. It's the perfect analogy for the two sides of this town.

I could keep going into much more detail about all the individual shops (and there are many more) but why rob you of your own joy of discovery? If you have a free day and it's sunny out, or even if it's cloudy and god-awful dreary, go to Poulsbo's downtown, explore for half the day and be disgustingly happy. Oh, and remember to keep the merchants there afloat-- they really appreciate the business.

BREMERTON, WA

Bremerton has a long history of being what was known at the turn of the century as a "wide-open town." Or, as local historian B.E. Schureman reported, a "heyday for crime, graft and immoral enterprises." Needless to say, Bremerton has changed a bit, although perhaps not as much as its town fathers would have hoped.

Bremerton began as a speculation. When the town's namesake, William Bremer, heard rumors of the US Navy looking at suitable locations for its new naval shipyard, he jumped at the opportunity. Bremer convinced his brother-in-law, Henry Hansel, to buy some unimproved wilderness along the Sinclair Inlet hoping for a potential payoff. The gambit worked, though not at first. The Bremer brothers bought the acreage that now forms downtown Bremerton from a mysterious homesteader named Andrew Williams for the then-tidy sum of $200 per acre. Seven months later, the Navy purchased a large part of that land for the new shipyard, for the bargain rate of $50 an acre. Bremer understood that selling at a loss to the Government made sense as long as you control the land surrounding the base. That's where he and his brother cleaned up.

Although "cleaned up" may be a poor choice of words. They certainly did well financially, but the type of businesses that are eager to be close to a new Naval facility fall under two categories; housing and entertainment. Namely, sailors need places to live and somewhere to blow off steam after a long shift of building up America's fighting force at sea. Bremer sold to the Navy at a discount but made a mint in the surrounding areas, parceling the land out and making hundreds of dollars per acre. Around the base rose up every manner of "immoral" enterprise; saloons, gambling houses, brothels. You name it, they had it. Every young sailor or worker sent to the Pacific Northwest base came back home drunk, penniless, and with an unwelcome tingle in the nether regions that never quite disappeared.

Eventually, the matter came to the attention of the Secretary of the Navy, who'd been all but forced to notice that a goodly amount of Bremerton sailors needed reforming. In 1902, he threatened to close the base down if Bremerton didn't get its act together, and soon. Of course, this sent the fledgling mayor and city council into a panic, enacting strict anti-liquor laws, popular with some residents and the Navy, but not necessarily with the patrons--that is, the sailors.

As nationwide prohibition would show later on a larger scale, keeping alcohol inaccessible verges on the impossible. You work hard, want a good time and a few drinks to blow off steam, chances are, someone is going to find a way to give it to you. Within a few years of the reforms, Bremerton was back to its old tricks. Saloons popped up all over, although less conspicuous this time around.

The criminal reputation of Bremerton became local lore thanks to the singular focus of its residents. As early as March 1906, a local watering hole named Jack Smith's Louvre Saloon burned to the ground. A local youth, A.D. Humble, a teenage firefighter who would become the town's first fire chief, was quoted saying, "The saloon burned down, but we did manage to save most of the whiskey." Of course they did.

Every mayor had their own way of dealing with the problems, some more colorful than others. Mayor Jack McGillivray ran a blacksmith shop on Second Street before he was elected mayor. Once elected, he decided it was time to clean up the streets, with a sledgehammer. As McGillivray tells it, "The first place we hit was a gambling house run by a fellow named Bulldog Kelly. I knocked on the door and he opened a sliding panel and peaked out at us. When he saw who it was, he told us he was running according to the law. ... I patted the sledgehammer and told him as far as he was concerned, it was the law." But even these heroic tactics had little effect on the town, and the good times kept rolling on.

As the national mood tempered, so did the town of Bremerton. The Navy retained its naval base, and the town moved on from the bawdy reputation, though some elements of that stigma remain.

KINGSTON, WA

Kingston is a place most Washingtonians have visited once, though not necessarily on purpose, perhaps noting the town's sleepy and modestly comfortable nature. Due to easy ferry access from Edmonds, Kingston is a quick way to get to the Olympic Peninsula if you are traveling from Whatcom or Snohomish county, rather than driving all the way around through Tacoma over the Narrows Bridge. I can't blame anyone for wanting to avoid driving through Tacoma.

Most people, however, don't know about Kingston, and that's exactly how the residents want to keep it. It's a town where they notice new additions right away and only care for a modest amount of tourism. Thankfully, many of the thousands passing through each year are too focused on deadlines and smartphones to recognize the beauty around them. They must pass right through, thinking to themselves "Oh, this is nice," before slamming on the brakes in traffic, swearing, and moving along. The locals would rather they stopped and bought a coffee or some postcards, of course, but as long as tourists and passers-by don't move in next door, all is well.

Kingston, like so many towns in the area, had a different name upon its creation. Founded in 1853 by a tree feller named Benjamin Bannister, Kingston was first known as Appletree Cove. The thought behind this name is something of a mystery. The area is not blessed with an abundance of apple trees, nor are apples (or the trees that bear them) a significant feature of Western Washington. One can assume that Bannister, in a desperate search for quality names, or perhaps a fit of whim, randomly decided that Appletree Cove sounded pleasant enough. He was right, of course, and the town's population grew.

In 1878, a young entrepreneur named Michael King bought a local cabin on Appletree Cove and began a prosperous logging business. Cutting down trees is big business in Washington and his enterprise grew, forcing him to build several shacks and bunkhouses to accommodate the growing staff of loggers. Unfortunately, the souring local economy forced King to abandon his operation, leaving the shacks and houses intact. Drifters, squatters, and the random logger occupied the empty cabins. They formed a ramshackle community that the locals jokingly referred to as King's Town. Of course, the name stuck.

Several years later, a wealthy hotelier named Charles C. Calkins dreamed of adding a beautiful resort to his growing empire of hotels. His first choice was Appletree Cove. The land itself had everything going for it to be successful. It boasted of a deep port capable of handling vessels of all sizes, a pleasant countryside, some of the finest beachsides in Puget Sound, and proximity to a growing urban population looking for a retreat. There was no way it could fail, but that's exactly what happened. Calkins quickly plotted the land, making plans for a grand hotel, a boat launch, a classically rural church on the hill, and even a college. The setup was perfect. Except that no one wanted to live next to the shanty town of Kingston. Calkins ambitious plans failed and he abandoned the town a few years later.

As is often the case, a town's history shows the way for its future. Kingston has never been an up-and-coming metropolis or even a hidden gem. It's simply a small town with a lot of charm and character. Always has been.

Dubbed the "Little City by the Sea", a title that might be a tad ambitious, Kingston has slowly become a big fish in a little pond and, as mentioned before, the gateway to the Olympic Peninsula from the north. It also has its fair share of vacation and summer homes, fulfilling a part of Calkins' dream, which gives it a busy air in summer and peaceful slumber in the winter months.

In short, it's probably someplace I would move if I did not have to work in a city.

PORT TOWNSEND, WA

The one thing you notice upon entering Port Townsend's downtown is that it is pleasantly old. Not old in the sense of being broken and needing to be replaced immediately, but more of the "they don't build 'em like that anymore" variety. With its fine, surprisingly pristine Victorian buildings and a vibrant artistic culture, Port Townsend seems content with itself, but happy to embrace the many tourists that pass through.

But there's also a prevalent sense of loss on every buttress and handsome piece of scroll work, like the town could have been more, greater, important. In fact, it nearly was.

Somewhere around 1870, great things were in store for Port Townsend. Named after George Vancouver's favorite Marquis, the small, bustling town was on track to be the next major city in the Northwest. The port handled a majority of goods coming from Asia into the Northwest, so the town's prospects grew with each passing day. All the town needed to cement its place in history was a major railroad connection from the east to carry more goods to eager customers across the country. Only then would Port

Townsend's future be assured.

Fate intervened as depression wracked the nation. The railroads barely had enough money to lay their tracks to the Puget Sound, much less through some complicated geography to Port Townsend. As the money ran dry around Tacoma, and later Seattle, the proprietors decided against spending more money to make good on their promises of expansion. The dream of a major port of call in Port Townsend crashed, with no chance of rescue. With the lack of prospects decided, the speculators, tradesmen, and investors that had so eagerly crowded the city's streets in hopes of riches left in droves, like having the wind knocked out of you by a heavyweight boxer. It took 80 years for the town to catch its breath again.

In a curious way, all those speculators leaving in such a hurry was a blessing for the town. While other local townships enthusiastically demolished their beautiful Victorian relics for modern concrete tributes to practicality and aesthetic horror, Port Townsend was stuck in perpetual Victorian sta- sis--architecturally speaking at least. The buildings aged, but no one came and told the friendly but now limited townsfolk that they needed to be replaced with something much more functional and much less visually appealing.

So the old buildings stayed and aged with grace.

Of course, even grace has limits. As Port Townsend's downtown began to crumble through years of neglect, the townsfolk gave serious thought to replacing their unique structures. Then, in the 1970's, someone had the fortunate revelation that it would be a remarkable shame if they replaced all those buildings with the communist dream of soaring concrete towers. They lobbied the state and established the buildings as landmarks, solidifying Port Townsend's wonderful Victorian heritage.

I thought about all this history on the drive up with my wife and son. It was my birthday, it was a weekend, and I got a bug to visit Port Townsend. My wife happily agreed. The drive up to Port Townsend from our house in Port Orchard is almost worth the trip on its own. Driving along highway 19, the road takes you into Beaver Valley and some of the most picturesque scenery in the world. It's quintessentially pastoral with its valley greens and yellows, blissful in its peace and quiet. Not for the first time, I wished for a small fortune so I could buy the entire valley and preserve it forever before someone decides to make a quick buck and build a golf course or ticky-tack housing developments. I sighed several times as we drove along, my wife smiling at my contentedness.

Entering Port Townsend from the highway is a study in preparations. The main drag curves and teases you while you long to see the downtown. The winding road, where Highway 20 turns into West Sims, tricks you into believing that maybe, just perhaps, you took a wrong turn. Several unsightly strip malls line the road, and by the time I reached a large parking lot with a Safeway grocery, I was nearly convinced that I had somehow missed the real Port Townsend.

If you soldier on, as we did, you will be well rewarded by the old Victorian grandeur, suddenly but pleasantly rising before you. There are few whole towns as big as Port Townsend with these types of buildings still standing. I could imagine how impressive the place must have seemed one hundred and twenty years ago. We made a loop through the main downtown strip. I fought the urge I always have when driving through a downtown of sticking my head out and looking up at the tops of buildings. The main drag held a surprising amount of people coming and going in the many shops, at least, more than I expected on a cold and rainy Sunday in January.

We circled around and found a nice parking lot at the edge of town, deciding to attack the shops from one side of the street and come back down the other. The first thing I noticed about Port Townsend was the air of tourism, but not in any standard way. Most tourist traps are replete with candy shops, souvenir stores, and garage sales pretending to be "antique" stores. Port Townsend has these too, though not in quantity. It has something more: a sense that people actually live there. It's almost as if they like living there, and that they would like you to pass through, leave a bit of money, and take some fine memories with you. I've never seen a more agreeable tourist trap.

You know that people like living in a place when they put their local touch in ways that are not meant for the touristy masses. Port Townsend has these touches in spades: small, underground speak-easy-style restaurants, found only upon careful inspection, side streets that open up to adorable and inviting cafes. I imagined that weeks of study would not afford me the necessary opportunity to explore all the town's secrets.

Down the main street and around the corner was a rather curious bookstore called the Writer's Workshoppe. I typically frown on stylistic spellings of words, as they almost always lead to the proprietor being on the snootier side of life. But the name intrigued me and I have an odd but strong compulsion to enter every bookstore I see. Inside, books lined every wall to the ceiling, providing that agreeable smell that gently used books make. Upon closer inspection, I noticed the unique organization of their books. Instead of your typical subject categories like "mystery" or "Sci-fi", the Workshoppe rejected common wisdom and instead organized by top 100 lists. They had lists such as "Top 100 books of All Time," "Top 100 Books to Read When You Need to Smile," or "Top 100 Books to Scare Your Pants Off". Whether these were actually the top 100 of anything is up to taste, but I thought it was an excitingly inventive way to shake up book browsing.

We walked to the back and I saw some meeting rooms with people discussing poetry. I can write prose (on my good days), but poetry has always been completely beyond my abilities. The order, the cadence, the imagery, and the ability to condense it all is too much to keep in my mind at once. I appreciate anyone who can create, or even honestly appreciate good poetry. The wall displayed a list of similar events for writers of all types. I realized the name 'Writer's Workshoppe' was apt (still stylized, but forgiven), as it is more a writing incubator than a regular bookstore.

Reluctantly, my family dislodged me from the bookstore and we continued exploring. Just down the street, my wife handed me her camera so that I could snap a picture of her and our son. I say "her camera" because it would be pointless for me to own one. The only camera I own is on my phone and that's only because I didn't have an option not to include it. All this to say that I have the unerring ability to take, without a trace of doubt, the absolute most boring pictures in existence. As a rule, they are never good. They live on that fine line of passable, which means the subject is often free of blur, but the picture is not remarkable. I've seen others, namely my wife and her sister, that have the visual acuity necessary for stunning photography. They can tilt and focus in such a way that the result is a moment captured in time, something to be saved and cherished. Mine are forgotten immediately. So when I say that my wife gave me her camera, you understand her lack of options. After a significant amount of instruction, the pictures were taken and nothing was left to do about them. They were good enough.

Being January in Washington State, the day was slate gray, cold, with a hint of rain in the air. What impressed me was the sheer number of people walking around. They all moved with a quiet, contented energy as if they could meander and march in the same step. All of the natives were kindly and smiling, as if meeting us and saying 'Hi' was the best thing in the world. I was charmed by everyone.

We walked by a shop which pulled my wife, by her inner being, through its doors. Not wanting to stand awkwardly on the sidewalk, I followed inside.

It was one of those eclectic, vintage, perfumed type shops that always leave me at a loss about what to do. As she disappeared into the multitudes of lace and swirls, I could either follow her around or strike out on my own. Both possibilities presented considerable challenges. I chose not to follow her and wandered around the shop. I noticed right away that if I happened to stop and look at anything, there was no possibility that it could be seen as anything but slightly creepy. A man standing in a store filled with items for women, his nervous eyes darting around as he handles some Sterling silver earrings can look nothing but odd. I kept moving, unintentionally shark-like in my maneuvers, but amid the rhinestone earrings and multi-textured scarves, nothing seemed worth looking at. Nor did it seem prudent to do so. Mostly, when I go in these stores I simply try to keep moving and stay inconspicuous.

On my twelfth pass by the scarves, I noticed the shop had a large supply of small wooden signs with "fun" and quirky sayings. They littered every spare corner. If there was a free or bare patch, a sign was there to fill it. The one rule that every sign seemed to follow was that it must be inexcusably trite. From "believe and achieve" to the sage wisdom of "be patient: god isn't finished with me yet," and even "don't mind this stupid sign, it doesn't mean anything anyway." I wondered about the kind of person who bought these signs and thought, "I've been looking for a sign that says 'food is good' for my kitchen. My life is now complete!" Many of the signs were obviously designed for the meanest of spirits cloaked in a "just kidding" attitude. How else would you read the sign "Lord, if I can't be skinny, at least make all my friends fat"? Ha ha, I hope you develop an eating disorder, become overweight, then get diabetes and die, ha ha, just kidding. Mercifully, my wife made her purchases and we left before I mentioned any of this to the proprietor.

Shortly after exiting, the rain started in earnest and we decided to leave. I was thankful. Port Townsend has a beautiful soul, wonderful apportioned with Victorian sensibility and design, but no amount of charm can make me cheerful in cold, windswept rain.

PORT ORCHARD, WA

No one knows where Port Orchard is located. They sort of intuitively know, but not in reality. When I tell people where I lived, they have a look of strained comprehension on their face, like I just asked them to do a piece of complicated math. Eventually, they nod their heads but I can tell they have already made the decision that my former home is unimportant.

And they are not completely wrong about that fact. It's not important to know where to find Port Orchard unless you actually live there. Port Orchard isn't quite in the middle of nowhere but it's far enough away from large groups of people that it definitely has a rural feel. The town represents a fine cross between suburban-concrete chic and a scary backwoods where moonshine and banjos are a staple. What it lacks in shootouts and police chases, it more than makes up for in awkward suburban sprawl and cars in front yards on blocks. It's a curious place to live, an incomplete getaway from the hustle and bustle of modern life.

I'm never sure how to fully describe Port Orchard, mainly because it's not even sure what it is yet.

The town began as a small port side community and just grew out from the shore, slowly, without much in the way of planning or thought. Something needed to be built, a grocery store, a Mexican restaurant, a Staples office supply store, well there was some land, let's build it. I'm sure the town folk were just happy to have a place to buy quality staplers. This haphazard style of urban un-planning led to a baffling lack of cohesion. This is evident in the many islands of retail coming out of nowhere and retreating just as quickly as you drive by.

The town has a rich history of confusion and lack of external recognition. Originally Port Orchard was named Sidney, after the patriarch of one of the founding fathers in the area. This name was short-lived, though, because within a year, Sidney was elected to become the county seat (with a courthouse and everything). To live up to its new status, the townsfolk wanted a name more majestic and indicative of the geography.

They decided to petition the state legislature to change from Sidney to Port Orchard, the name of the adjacent body of water. There was only one catch. Just north of the inlet, across from Sidney, a small village of Charleston had beat them to the punch and petitioned for the same name just months earlier. The state legislature denied Sidney its name change.

Unfortunately, no one told the federal Post Office. Charleston, while it petitioned the state legislature, failed to talk to any postal officials. The Sidney folks were more on-the-ball in this regard. A long-standing rule of any bureaucracy is to not look into matters too closely if it will cause a great deal of confusion. This is exactly what they did, establishing the Port Orchard post office for Sidney.

To make matters worse, when the builders came to construct the Port Orchard post office they were diverted to Charleston, now known to Washington State as Port Orchard. Once the Post Office Department realized the mistake, they placed the Charleston post office in Sidney for no clear reason, other than now no one was happy, which is just how the government likes it.

This unfortunate situation lasted for eleven years until in 1903. A young politician convinced the legislature that this specific type of screw up was not in the state's best interest. After several months of persuading, the Post Offices were changed and Sidney was renamed, officially now, Port Orchard. But by that time, the town's lack of respect and recognition was established, and locals have since wondered where Port Orchard is.

GIG HARBOR, WA

If you're driving along Highway 16 near Tacoma, you might have seen signs for Gig Harbor. You also might have thought to yourself "Now that sounds like a moderately pleasant place to live or visit."

Give yourself a pat on the back, you would be correct. Moderate, also known as bland, or nice, describes Gig Harbor to a "T."

Not completely devoid of charm, the town boasts of some wonderful features, but it's best not to expect too much. While Gig Harbor offers a large step up from its rather dismal neighbors, if you travel there expecting a rich garden of possibilities, expect disappointment.

A name like Gig Harbor conjures up images of a delightful little town. The streets are happy, well-tended, and lined with prosperous shops. The light is a little brighter and the townspeople people reflect that. In fact, type "Gig Harbor" in your favored search engine and you will find that it's one of the top five small towns in America, at least according to the to the Smithsonian. On the institution's website, you can read a long article about the many virtues of the sleepy Northwest town.

My comments in braces [ ].

"While Gig Harbor is known for its natural beauty, with the most scenic views of Mt. Rainier and the Puget Sound [Most scenic? Hardly. That honor goes to the Puyallup Valley. Though it pays for its glorious mountain views by being under constant threat of burial by mudslide if Mount Rainier suddenly decides to explode], it is the sense of healthy relationships and active living within the community that makes this city stand out ['active living' just sounds like an advertisement for a retirement community]. ... Annual events like concerts in the park, guided beach walks, outdoor cinema, maritime and lighted boat parades, dog walks, garden tours, and weekly art walks bring out hosts of volunteers and give residents a reason to get to know their neighbors [This person has obviously never been to Gig Harbor, where you only get to know your neighbors to compare your life to theirs and lord it over them, politely of course, if yours turns out to be better]. City planning has been strategic to preserve a healthy and creative way of life. Shopping centers and restaurants are available, but not cluttering every corner [Except for the unholy abomination that is Uptown]. Community gardens are cultivated with the help of local business sponsors and volunteers. Miles of shoreline, deep water bays, and scenic islands have made it famous for water sports, kayakers and boating [Fun Fact: one of those "scenic islands" is McNeil Island, a federal prison island now dedicated to housing child molesters. Water sports not recommended in its vicinity]. Bikers, walkers, and runners can be seen daily on the forest trails, including a 5-mile public paved trail called the Cushman, which hosts dramatic views. Artistic freedom is upheld and residents host concerts and art shows in their own homes and self-owned businesses [As opposed to places where artistic freedom is oppressed? What country is the Smithsonian writer from?]."

To understand the town, it helps to know a bit of its history. First of all, Gig Harbor is named after a dingy, or rather a small boat called, in days past, a gig. Not the most auspicious of beginnings but every town has to start somewhere. As township origin stories go, Gig Harbor, at least, begins with a little adventure on the high seas.

It was a dark and stormy night on the rough Puget Sound in late 1840. Captain Charles Wilkes was on a survey mission for the US Government to locate "islands and shoals of doubtful existence" and sought harbor in a small but pleasant (and calmer) body of water unknown to all but the local natives. The steep valley walls sheltered Wilkes and his men, saving them from a cold, wet swim to shore. They waited out the storm in the inlet and then made their way back to the ship. Much later, when publishing the official map of the Oregon Territory, Wilkes, used all of his great creative muscle and rewarded the tiny vessel that carried him to relative safety. He named the small inlet "Gig Harbor" and so it's forever been known. I imagine the name would have been a private joke between Wilkes and his men--that is if they were talking to him. To say that Wilke's men disliked their captain would be a gross understatement.

Wilkes himself was a fiendishly fiery and polarizing fellow. Orphaned, then raised by his aunt, he attended Columbia College as soon as he was of age, then quickly joined the US Navy as a midshipman in 1818. As he rose through the ranks, Wilkes proved himself adept at Naval Survey techniques. In 1838, he was chosen to lead the expedition into the great, less than satisfactorily charted Pacific Ocean. Taking his mission with no small amount of grisly enthusiasm, he sailed his men all over the Pacific. They visited Hawaii, Samoa, Australia, the Pacific Northwest, the Californian coast, Latin America, and then, just to top things off, circumnavigated the world. It took a little over 4 years but once completed, he had the satisfaction of being the last all-sail naval vessel to achieve such a task. It was quite an accomplishment and deserving of reward. Unfortunately for him, when his ship returned to New York, Wilkes was immediately taken into custody for a court martial.

The problem was that Charles Wilkes was not a man blessed with an overabundance of charm. What he lacked in social niceties he more than made up for in brutal discipline, fear tactics, and general jackassery. Thanks to his reckless antics, he lost an astounding 28 men and two ships, one of them due to sloppy disregard of the Columbia River sandbar. He also managed to piss off loads of people across the seven seas. The military charged Wilkes with 'illegally punishing' his men, a wrist slap to be sure. He was then banished to finish his report, a task he grudgingly dragged on for fifteen years, with full pay, until the outbreak of the Civil War. Since our country needed a man of his "talents" to lead the Union to victory, they called him into service once more.

The Tides Tavern, a local landmark and colorful watering hole, began its long life as a general store run by the improbably named Axel Uddenburg. The Tides is the perfect analogy for Gig Harbor - turn-of-the-century, remodeled, and slightly charming. The bar's history and traditions are evident from the memorabilia hanging on the walls by the hundreds. At first it seems self-serving, but observing the attention to detail and obvious affection the locals have for this landmark, the charm level ratchets up nicely.

One even learns a few interesting facts. Like the Tides was once called Three Finger Jack's, named after its notorious proprietor. Jack ran the place like his personal man cave. He sang with the band every night, drank with his friends, and generally lived it up through the 60's and 70's, back when you could do such things and still maintain a business. As the tavern's website puts it "The Tavern never made much money, but no one cared." Apparently Jack began to care around 1973 because he sold the bar to Peter Stanley and ran off to China, with a French prostitute named Dominique, to became a pirate. I may have embellished that last part, but once a guy named Three Fingered Jack sells his man cave bar, what else is there left for him to do?

Stanley has run the joint ever since and seems to be making a fine go of it. The food is decent, the service polite, and at no time would you mistake the Tides for a themed bar. If you want a good visual of the decor, think a maritime version of Applebee's. But the food is better and the crap on the walls is real crap, not hand selected to make you feel nostalgic. It's all quite nice.

Except for the parking lot, that is. The lot is small, narrow, with a slope approaching the vertical limits of usefulness. I can only imagine the look on people's faces if the lot is even a little icy, as they lose their footing and fly, tumbling head over feet, into the waiting harbor. A quick view of the parking lot on a Friday afternoon shows that most of the customers don't mind the danger. The Tides is the kind of place that people go to because they always have gone there, or because everyone else they know has gone there and they haven't chosen a new place to go. Its popularity also could be because the options in downtown Gig Harbor are preposterously limited.

I've driven through downtown Gig Harbor several times, and on each trip, I got the impression of a town with a sleepy soul. When visiting downtown Gig Harbor, the best course of action is to walk from one end to the other in order to soak up the local flavor. Walking from the Tides parking lot, you'll see the usual smattering of custom jewelry stores, antique boutiques, and local art houses that are legion in any smaller Washington city. They're the shops that carry gaudy designs, better suited to a soap opera-like conception of wealth than anything aesthetically appealing.

Down the main street is another local restaurant, not as time-tested as The Tides, but still a local hangout, named Spiros. I once had a business meeting in their makeshift meeting room and became intimately familiar with their way of doing business. The first thing you must understand about Spiros is that twelve-year-olds seem to run the place. Granted, I've found that once I reached my thirtieth birthday, anyone younger than 20 looks 12 to me, but the point is made. I arrived for my meeting 5 minutes early and announced my arrival to the hostess, whose wistfully bored expression instilled in me a healthy skepticism in her restauranting ability. She gave me the once-over and said, "Ya, it's not exactly ready yet. So you can wait here or something." I had no idea what the "or something" entailed, so I stood awkwardly by the door. Which I assume is what she meant.

Looking around the restaurant, I noticed a decided lack of customers. I asked the hostess if this was usual for a weekday and she responded, "How should I know." She phrased it as a statement, and I kept to myself from then on. As more members of my company arrived, they were also informed that the room was not ready and told to engage in "waiting or something" behavior.

Finally, the hostess (I can barely bring myself to call her that) informed us that the space was ready and ushered the seven of us into the room. The "meeting room" was simply the main dining room with regular dining tables sitting where you would imagine regular dining tables would sit in a restaurant, covered with white cloths and place settings. Nothing out of the ordinary seemed to have taken place to warrant an extra 15-minute wait. I asked where we were supposed to sit, and the hostess motioned around the room, "Wherever you want." I swear inside she added, 'Duh!"

My party sat and a deep resignation hung over us, like when you find yourself in the middle seat of a fully booked airplane. You're not happy about the situation, but you're already committed, and now there is nothing to do but suck it up and get through. Ten minutes after we sat down, a waitress showed up to pass out six glasses of water, never saying a word or making eye contact. I briefly considered the possibility that the sixth was a shared glass of some type, but I declined the opportunity and graciously gave my neighbor the glass in hopes that the waitress would be more attentive than the hostess. It was not meant to be. After ten more minutes the waitress came back, presumably to take our order, but I made the mistake of asking for an extra glass of water. She left to get it. Ten more minutes passed.

The service didn't improve throughout the meal. The food itself was nothing special, but at least the prices were exorbitant. I am thankful for one thing, though. My experience at Spiros gave me one useful tool for gauging the minimum quality of service I can expect from a restaurant. Look at the clocks. I noticed halfway through the meal that the clock above a doorway was off by an hour. My initial impulse was to inform the management, but I thought better of that immediately. Why waste my energies? If it's two months after daylight saving and your staff is too lazy (or incompetent) to change the time on your clocks, I can only imagine who you hired to cook my food.

I believe the clocks will sum it all up. I can forgive one person's inability to seat us (or address customers) properly, or a waitress that gives poor service, or a lack of accommodation to business needs, or even a lukewarm, poorly cooked meal. Each of these happens from time to time, but all at once is an epidemic easily spotted by a business's clocks. Trust me on this one.

Downtown Gig Harbor is quite walkable, and you can enjoy a leisurely stroll, if that's your thing, down the main thoroughfare. This is all assuming the weather in Washington State cooperates of course. Washington weather has an enthusiastic attachment to rain with a cold breeze that's just strong enough to make you wish that you stayed home.

While downtown Gig Harbor has some fine walking available, there is simply not enough of it. The main road is far too short, although quite scenic if the marina is your idea of a nice view. The one thing that I love is the perfect blend of forest evergreen with the still blue-gray water of the Puget Sound.

I could travel anywhere in the world, see great wonders of the world, but that glorious combination, especially when the summer sun kisses the water, will always fill my heart with a special type of happiness.

There are several small businesses lining the streets--the usual type of professional offices that hang a shingle in small towns. Doctors, dentists, insurance salesmen, lawyers and the like. One office was called Insurance Solutions and it represents an epidemic that I loathe: poor naming. In this case, it feels like a cop out.

I imagine a pudgy, grease-stained man sitting in a booth at Spiros, lamenting the bad service, trying to name his next venture into the field of private insurance. He couldn't name it after himself, as I imagine his name rhymes with something less-than-credible like stinky or crazy. So, as he browses the latest edition of the Wall Street Journal, he sees the word solutions mentioned over and over. "Solutions, huh?" he thinks to himself, a pervading laziness taking hold. "That's exactly what I provide!" he says out loud, perhaps a bit too enthusiastically, "I find solutions for insurance." Thus, a bad name was born. It's boring, it's uninteresting, and honestly it brings us all down as a species.

If you look closely at some of the tenant combinations in downtown, you might be left wondering if the lack of vacancy is due to exceedingly generous rents. One building, in particular, stood out. On one side was a permanent makeup shop, the kind where they tattoo your face so you always look your best. Or so they say. If you have ever met someone with a face tattoo of makeup--and you would remember if you did--the effect is not unlike the scariest, most insane clown you could conjure up in your worst imaginations. And yet, there are women who choose to do this on purpose. The shop is rather hopefully named "Forever Young".

On the other side of this building was 'A Better Life Counseling Center.' My immediate question was if the counselors, seeing the permanent makeup shop, perceived a built-in market for their services. Or perhaps the proprietors at Forever Young were only concerned with the cheap rent, and some possible kickbacks on the counseling fees. I have yet to find out.

Down the street a bit is another odd collection of stores. The best is a survivalist shop.

For those that may not be familiar with such places, and I do not pretend to be an expert, survivalist shops help prepare you for the end of days, or the near approximation. They sell everything one would need for the coming apocalypse, namely the fall of the United States when the government decides to suspend all freedoms and turn us into communists. I read on the internet, and they can't post this on the internets if it's not true, that the end of our whole way of life has been imminent for years now. Seeing as people feel this way, several smart people thought to themselves, "I bet we could make a lot of money on these folks." And so they could, and do, quite a bit actually. They sell everything a survivalist would need, from tents to flashlights, to waterproof matches, backpacks--basically, everything you need to go camping but better and more expensive. All this is chicken feed compared to the real grift. Food.

These businesses sell lots of food that will supposedly keep for years at a time. That might not sound like a promising enterprise, but it's all in the marketing. They don't sell just a week's worth of food, they sell five years or more, with a convenient payment plan of course. Popular conservative talk show hosts hype these products all the time so I imagine that business has never been better. The store itself is rather sparse--it's more of a showroom and education center. They order the goods to be delivered to the consumers. When the government collapses and the zombies take over, you don't want to have to run down to the local survival store for your rations. Shipped to your door is the only way to go.

Gig Harbor's odd penchant for combining disparate types of retail ventures reaches its zenith in a small shop in the middle of town. As soon as you see the sign for the Java and Clay Cafe, you have no choice but to go inside. This combination would never occur to me, not even if you placed a cup of joe and an unfinished pot in my lap, pointed meaningfully and raised your eyebrows in that way that indicates I'm falling behind in the conversation. You could wait for years, waving your arms at the coffee and pottery in my now warm lap, and it wouldn't come to me. It's just not a business combination that my mind would consider a good match.

Once inside, though, somehow the mix of coffee and pottery clay goes together. Not exactly like peanut butter and jelly, but in an oddly pleasant way. The only unsettling surprise is the odor. It's impossible to describe the scent of coffee and pottery clay without saying it smells like you would imagine, but not as good. Let's say it would fail spectacularly as a house scent.

Downtown Gig Harbor is more or less pleasant, and light years better than the "other Gig Harbor", Uptown.

Uptown Gig Harbor is less a natural outgrowth of the town than a retail opportunity and practicality. Gig Harbor, the body of water, lies at the bottom of a rather steep valley, so the real estate opportunities, as for most bays, are limited and people start building inland. As people relocated, or rather fled, from Tacoma to Gig Harbor, the houses stretched farther away from downtown and away from the commercial center. As often happens, real estate developers saw more profit in building a new commercial center than propping up the old hub of commerce. So they erected a California-Style shopping experience (read: open mall and sprawling) that looks like a strip mall trying hard to look nice.

If you travel up the hill from downtown, you can muse on the delicious naming trickery of Uptown. Not only is 'up' more satisfying than 'down' (in most situations), but it also signifies being above everyone else, and plays into a whole host of silly psychological programming. It was a fine pick for a name. Yet, Gig Harbor's scenic downtown is struggling because of this short-sighted need to make a buck.

The problem is that Uptown is, in its deepest heart of hearts, heartless. A soulless suburban retail complex aspiring to look and feel nouveau-riche, merely serving the many shopping needs of locals who don't want to drive 20 minutes to the Tacoma Mall. But it serves in the most harmful way possible. The developers of Uptown had a blank canvas and they chose to paint with a bunch of parking lots and shops with pretentious names like Plum, Ayurvedic, etc. They are the kind of stores that buy cheap clothing made in Asia and sell them for expensive prices, Pier One knock offs for 50% more, and they all smell like cheap perfume and patchouli, the kind of smell that clings to your clothes, but with no discernible point of origin, as if they always smelled that way.

The only place with any semblance of local flair or promise is a small grocery called Harbor Greens. They're tiny, dedicated, and exceedingly happy to see your business. But, if your best experience in a town is the small grocery store and even that is a middling thrill, then you know it is time to leave.

PURDY, WA

If an out-of-state visitor hears the name Purdy, Washington, there're only two interpretations. The first is an unfortunate speech impediment that renders the speaker unable to pronounce the word "pretty" in reference to his or her feelings about the state's attractiveness. The second reason (and, obviously, the correct one) is that someone went to the trouble of naming a town in Washington Purdy. Originally, they did this with the best intentions, thinking only of the honor conferred on a helpful grocer by a grateful community.

In the 1880's, the land surrounding the town now called Purdy was in desperate need of a schoolhouse. A quirk in local geography prevented children from returning the way they came to school. Yes, that means they really did have to walk to school, uphill, both ways. Sometimes in the snow. Obviously, this situation was unsustainable and the town fathers issued a call to action. One of the founding fathers, Horace Knapp, stepped up, donating the acreage for a brand new schoolhouse on normal elevation. The actual materials for the schoolhouse building and furniture came from, Joseph W. Purdy, a grocer in

Tacoma, Washington. Purdy's only connection to the area that would one day bear his name was a pair of nephews with sob stories about grueling school day travels. In a fit of generosity, Joseph made sure the new schoolhouse was properly attended to.

While it was the salvation of many young feet, the simple building of a school house would not seem to warrant the naming of the town after the patron. Horace Knapp donated the land, and without that, the schoolhouse would have no place to dwell. Shouldn't Purdy be properly named Knapp? Sadly, history is curiously silent on the matter.

It would be a stretch to call Purdy a vacation destination.

In fact, it would be an incredible flexing of the truth. Purdy is mostly residential now, rolling hills and single family homes on polite and rather rural streets. But it does have one distinguishing feature that make it worth a stop and look-see: the Purdy bridge and spit. Spanning over Henderson Bay and marking the entrance to Burley Lagoon, the view from the bridge is quite pleasant, and during the summer the beach is one of the nicer spots to enjoy the all-too-brief two week Washington heatwave.

If you happen to be looking for Port Orchard on your way to cause some trouble in Bremerton, or returning from a fruitless search for Port Orchard (it's rather hard to find), Purdy is a sure to give you a modest thrill.

PORT HADLOCK, WA

When Samuel Hadlock set out on a wagon train in 1852 from his native New Hampshire to the prosperous land of Oregon, he had little idea that many years later, a town would happily bear his name. Not much is known about Samuel Hadlock, other than that he liked to cut down tall trees and turn them into planks for building. He did that quite well. Once he made the journey west, he worked his way through several mill towns until he was able to establish his own with the help of five friends. The Tacoma Mill was an immediate success and netted Sam a small fortune. But Sam wasn't happy to while away his days in Tacoma, Washington.

Hadlock sold his interest in the Tacoma Mill and purchased 362 acres of prime real estate south of Port Townsend. The area offered enough timber to last a lifetime of clear cutting and an easily accessible port from which he could transport the finished products. Life was grand. He built the mill into the largest lumber mill in the world, shooting out 150,000 board feet of lumber every day. It was quite the achievement.

Around 1910, the sawdust from the mill piled up

to the point that something had to be done. One of Hadlock's enterprising executives hit upon the idea of turning the wood waste into alcohol. Distilling wood into alcohol has been around since the Egyptians used the noxious liquid in their embalming processes. The problem with producing wood alcohol in massive quantities is you need quite a lot of wood or sawdust. Hadlock happened to have that in spades. They constructed an alcohol plant and began production, shipping alcohol locally at first.

It's important to know that you can't drink wood alcohol. Well, you can, but excessive or lasting consumption leads to blindness, comas, and then death. Not exactly a prime selling point, and ultimately a turn-off. It wasn't until later that wood alcohol, called methanol, was found to be a fine addition to many chemical processes.

The other advantage is that methanol is highly volatile, meaning that as an explosive it could be used with great effectiveness. But the very thing that made it desirable, its fantastic ability to blow everything up, made it a challenge to transport and use, especially with other more inert competitors. That left drinking the stuff, and the good people of Washington quickly found that drinking methanol versus drinking ethanol were rather different experiences. One made you throw up, the other made you dead.

The Hadlock alcohol plant closed in 1913, a victim of cruel government intervention after several methanol deaths. Alas for bright ideas.

Since those more interesting times, the lumber mill burned down, the alcohol plant was turned into a first class resort, and everyone moved up the hill away from the barren wreck of the lumber mill. Life moves at a slower pace now, and that's the way they like it.

OLYMPIA, WA

My buddy Mike wanted to take pictures of the ground. I didn't know why since, as I have mentioned, I have no photographic talents whatsoever, but he seemed excited about it so I thought I'd tag along. He had never been to Olympia, so I suggested we check it out.

Mike and I thought that since the capitol was right off the freeway, it would be the best first stop. Mike had never seen the capitol building and since he has an appreciation for older architecture, it would be a wonderful education. It was a nice thought at least, but the state had different ideas.

Apparently, to park at or near the state capitol building, you need a form of telepathy, or geolocation, like the kind birds use, to magically know where the visitor parking is located. They don't make it obvious. Your first entrance into the capitol grounds is a lovely, manicured park on both sides of the road, but no actual parking available--at least, none that isn't reserved for lobbyists or people who sleep with legislators. That is what I assume, since it's certainly not for the public.

The employee parking stretches past a roundabout. The magnificent statue in the center only taunts those trying their best to find somewhere to park where the police won't tow your car. I can attest that there are several parking lots near the beautiful, massive buildings on the legislative campus, but none of them are for the public. They all have recessed signs, positioned far enough into the lots so as to make turning around a common occurrence, that ban the public from parking between their inviting lines. Turning around once more, I tried to exit the campus in disgust and finally struck gold.

After navigating through the unfriendly spiderweb of poorly labeled employee parking, I finally saw a visitor parking lot off to the side of a building at the edge of the legislative campus. It was down a sketchy road that looked long forgotten, and across a back alley. Upon further inspection, they also charge you an exorbitant fee to park there. We decided that paying to park to see some old buildings was not in our best interest, though this is no doubt part of the legislator's plans. Why make it easy to park when you can make it difficult and expensive for the public and then not have to deal with them? Quite brilliant in its villainy.

So, off we went to the downtown of Olympia, which is where we wanted to go anyway. Not having any idea where to park, or even what we should be seeing, I parked near some closed up shops down by the marina. Of course, the parking wasn't free. It never is.

We exited the car and Mike immediately found some interesting ground to take photos of. I can't say that I saw the appeal immediately, but once he showed me his pictures, I was sold. He had the unerring ability to see brilliant compositions where I would see a bit of rust or a smattering of moss. Content that the day wouldn't be wasted, we made our way to the pier down the street. I appreciated the slow pace as I waited for Mike to photograph yet another tangled bit of roots poking through the cement because it gave me a chance to appreciate the odd composition of Olympia.

The view from the downtown is dominated by the massive capitol building on the hill, overlooking the entire town. What's interesting is that its presence was not a sure thing, even after the state was formed.

While Olympia was the chosen location for the territorial capital, its status as state capital was far from certain. Washington held a statewide vote to choose its next capital and many cities fought for the honor; Vancouver, Steilacoom, Seattle, Port Townsend, and Tacoma. One of the fiercest rivalries, though, was between the cities of Ellensburg and

Yakima.

Olympia was the logical choice for capital, but by the mid-1880s, both North Yakima and Ellensburg also had booming populations. Their busy Northern Pacific Railroad depots offered ease of travel and potential connection to possible future railroad lines. North Yakima, foreseeing the upcoming statehood, tried to claim the capital by legislative action during the 1887-1888 territorial session and was defeated by just one vote, largely thwarted by efforts from Ellensburg.

The public relations extravaganza that followed was breathtaking in its creative use of the truth. The editor of The Kittitas Standard, an Ellensburg newspaper, argued that the central location of Ellensburg in the 'most strikingly beautiful, unsurpassably healthy, admirably watered and immeasurably fertile, compact body of agricultural land of any extent on the North Pacific slope' made it the firm choice for the next state capital. Yakima had a different take.

The North Yakima newspaper, The Washington Farmer, published this spirited rant:

"There is but one point besides North Yakima that is in the race, and that is Ellensburg -- which is twice as high above the sea as North Yakima, therefore it is cold and frosty. Ellensburg is in a valley so narrow it is practically a canyon, and through it sweeps the icy blasts from the snow towering mountains that make the locality one of the most disagreeable and unhealthy in the world -- There is no possibility of any branch line of road ever being built from Ellensburg to any other point for the simple fact is that the surrounding rugged mountains form impossible barriers with no signs of a pass through them. The streets of Ellensburg are narrow without a hotel, or running water, and there is not a lawn, or a plot of grass, nor a garden in the village. There are five times as many saloons as North Yakima, and the court dockets show that the criminal classes prevail to a greater degree than they do in King County."

In order to entice the vote to Ellensburg further, Brittain and Samuel Craig built a prospective governor's mansion. Northwest Magazine reported that "Mr. Craig is putting up the finest brick residence on Capitol Hill in plain view of the city and when somebody asked him the other day if that was the Governor's mansion, he said it was. Whether some future governor of the state will reside there or not is an open question."

The structure was three stories with a four-story attached octagonal tower and made of brick. Although its tower was slightly suggestive of a castle tower, the mansion failed to impress beyond the city borders. In 1930, the building was remodeled as an apartment house and given a fantasy castle theme complete with a crenelated roofline and battlements.

Olympia is a city stuck between several decades like it has yet to make up its mind about what it wants to be when it grows up, or even if it's set on growing up at all. There are stores that look alarmingly like western saloons, complete with a century of neglect, next to poured concrete monoliths, the kind architects got so excited about in the 70's, next to modern buildings of the kind that look like random sized boxes stacked by an eight-year-old who has a touch of epilepsy. Across the street from us was the pier, but also a chain tire store, a senior center, which itself was next to a yoga studio/craft beer store. I had a hard time wrapping my head it all.

The docks, named Percival Landing (one would think a more exciting name could be discovered), are rather new, nice looking, and seem well-taken-care-of. A new playground sits in the distance next to one of those newer buildings, so common in the northwest, that tries hard to blend Asian influence with contemporary modernism. It always ends up looking decent but unremarkable. We walked the dock and Mike took more pictures of the ground, the wooden pier, basically anything pointed downward. He was having a great time, so I explored the area a bit and left him to his happy picture taking.

A plaque next to the pier railing reminded me of an interesting phenomena, rather unique to the Puget Sound in the late 19th century called the Mosquito Fleet. Because the land was too dense for travel, filled with millions of trees, which was perfect for the timber industry but rather inconvenient for transportation, the Puget Sound waterway was the easiest way to transport goods. Thanks to the cheapness of water transport, a small industry of steamboats grew to a considerable size, eventually swarming through the water, earning the nickname the Mosquito Fleet.

Actually, the plaque added some color to the story. It stated that the Mosquito Fleet got its name from an anonymous, but obviously older, curmudgeon, who looked out onto the beauty of the Puget Sound and saw his beloved water clogged with steamboats supplying the lifeblood of the region. According to historians, and who can deny them this, the Mosquito Fleet earned its nickname because this older, dissatisfied landowner explained, "Looks like a bunch of damned mosquitoes out there!" And so history was born.

While Mike busied himself with yet another picture of the dirt and pavement, I noticed a distinct pattern in the patrons of Percival Landing. It seemed to be the hot local spot for older immigrants, testing the rapidly diminishing capacities of their aging bodies, for middle-aged female speed walkers trying to work out enough to fit into their workout clothes, and young-ish men bitching about their first or second ex-wife and trying to hit on the speed walkers. More than once I heard a reference to "my damn ex" almost immediately followed by some half-assed attempt to hit on the middle-aged next ex-wife.

The "landing" is also littered with the oddest assortment of modern art that I just don't understand. One memorable piece consisted of scraps of metal, thrown together in order to represent a dog, or rather what I imagine a child's version of a dog would be if you gave that child several scraps of metal and a blowtorch. The other pieces are obviously taken from video games, though I'm not cool enough these days to know which ones. They all have that floaty, ethereal quality that modern games seem to enjoy, and look as if they will help you level up if you happen to touch them. Unfortunately, this was not the case.

The pier looked attractive and clean, but rather sterile. It looked as if it could have been a joyful and happy place, but a committee composed of older men who never intended to use the pier themselves decided firmly against it. That's how you get a lovely and jaunty sign that says, "Welcome Boaters" on a fence, behind a hedge, in a place where boaters would never, ever see it. Across the water is a Soviet-style building complete with poured concrete and water stains. The junky eyesore would be right at home in a Chernobyl wasteland. The well-maintained park surrounding it doesn't help the building look any better, in fact, it might make it worse. It's like an ugly haircut after someone has gone to the trouble of getting a facelift.

Mike finished with the pier, though how he knew that, I'll never know. He seemed to have an intuitive sense of when the area was fresh out of downward material to photograph. We proceeded into town, dodging traffic that was not keen on stopping for pedestrians and walked past a paid parking lot named "Park and Lock." It was an honest title, and reminder, since the lot itself looked like it was frequented by less reputable elements, and often.

The saloon-looking building was around the corner and I was happy to see it up close, as it had the most amazing name; The Rusty Rooster. It sounded like a dirty sex act, but upon closer inspection it was just an antique store. The full name, according to the window display was Rusty Rooster--Gifts and Jazzy Junk. Unfortunately, it was closed, so were not able to fully test the jazziness of its junk. A peek through the main window showed its wares to be haphazard and disorganized, like a slightly-less-disgusting hoarder house. It did look like there could have been a herd of feral cats nesting among the lampshades in the corner.

Down the street, we made another turn onto 4th Street and the world transformed before our feet. Suddenly, attractive shops lined the streets, all promising wholesome adventure and robust shopping opportunities. On closer inspection, each shop had an exceptional quirkiness, like a children's glass figurine museum and old time malt shop/soda fountain/teriyaki restaurant. But the signs and visage held a quaint 1950's charm that seemed to make the quirk work.

Mike and I ambled down the sidewalk, looking in different directions, and a man walking behind what must have been his sister-wives squeezed past us. As we made eye contact, he gave me the manly, obligatory head nod but no greeting. It's not that I wanted to stop and chat, but I have been noticing more of this behavior lately. When did it become proper not to greet someone out loud? You can convey a large amount of dignity when you greet someone with a kind word. Instead, men give each other a shallow head nod, often accompanied by a tightening of the lips. It's as if we are apologetic for the gesture. Stop it. I'd rather you greet me with a jaunty (and slightly embarrassing) 'AHOY!' than a silent, thin-lipped nod. Although I should allow that perhaps this man's tongue was whipped into submission by his polyamorous ways. You know how sister-wives can be.

Across the street, staring at these perfect and quirky shops is a patch of ill-kept land that looks like the dirty backyard of a low-budget frat. A waist-high chain link fence surrounded the property but it had seen better days. In the back was an unoccupied building with more structural problems than a second grader's grammar. Off to the side of the property was an old Volvo, wearing an air of use but not confirming that suspicion. The rest of the yard was littered with the following: untended raised gardens (for growing weeds, it seemed), an old truck tire, broken chicken coop, newish dog house for a medium sized dog, charcoal grill, an old boombox radio hanging from a tree branch, rusted metal gazebo, and one brand new traffic cone, lying on its side near the Volvo. Also scattered among the various items were several types of chairs, some standing upright and others tossed on their sides. There was a No Trespassing sign displayed prominently on the back, but I could tell it seemed disheartened to be so thoroughly ignored. Mike and I stood in front of the chain link for a full minute trying to fathom what happened there but came up blank. Sometimes you have to leave things to mystery and let them be.

Every turn downtown reveals one of the many personalities of Olympia. Does it want to be historic? Modern? Everything to all people? I don't know for sure. What I do know is that there are parts of downtown Olympia where it looks entirely safe to urinate publicly without anyone caring or noticing. It looks like many do just that. What baffles me about Olympia is that those parts abut the newish ones where all the women wear yoga pants and short hats with ponytails and carry Starbucks everywhere. They seem separate and mingled all at the same time, but in a haphazard, non-cohesive way.

One great virtue of Olympia is its vagrant population. At first, I was taken aback, because if Olympia has one thing in abundance, it's homeless people. As Mike and I walked along, I marveled at how content they all looked, happy even. Sure, they wore old, dirty clothes and rocked the non-showered look like it was fashion week, but always with a serene, placid look on their faces. It made me wonder what they were putting in the water.

The thing that most amazed me, though, and Mike and I didn't realize this until we were on our way back to the car, was that not once were we propositioned for money. I rarely carry hard currency anymore, so it is easy to shrug my shoulders and tell most panhandlers that I can't help. That was not necessary in Olympia where, apparently, they had everything they needed. It was refreshing, actually.

As walked back to the car, a lady in a severe

outfit, the kind women wear when they are trying to be taken seriously in business but also keep an edge, walked by us. She looked in our direction, nodded, and winked, with a knowing smile. It was like we were now part of her club. In a way, we were, and I decided that being in Olympia's special club was not so bad at all.

PORT LUDLOW, WA

Charles Wilkes, the enthusiastically brutal and intemperate Captain of the United States Exploring Expedition who named Gig Harbor after a dingy, also had the fortune of naming several other locations in Puget Sound, including Port Ludlow. Since naming is hard work, less creative individuals rely on handy ways of cheating, namely using the names of dead soldiers and sailors. Usually, the names chosen have some major significance, but at times, they are obscure references. Such is the case with Augustus C. Ludlow.

Ludlow was a lieutenant in the United States Navy and second in command under Captain James Lawrence on the USS Chesapeake. Ludlow's major claim to fame is being killed, along with his Captain, in a sea battle with the HMS Shannon on June of 1813, during the War of 1812. He was then buried, for reasons unknown, with the captain and the captain's widow in New York. History is silent on the details of Ludlow's skills or abilities, leaving us to wonder what Wilkes saw in such a man. Perhaps his name was on a list, and it was conveniently next to Wilkes' finger.

Ludlow's ship, the USS Chesapeake, was built as a result of the Naval Act of 1794. It was one of the first six original frigates created to be the chief capital ships of the fledgling US Navy. Originally intended to be a 44 gun ship, due to shortages and poor planning, the design was down a bit to 38 guns. Some things never change. The USS Chesapeake was famous for starting the War of 1812 when, rather than be boarded by a British frigate looking for deserters, the commanding officer, James Barron, decided it was a much better idea to open fire on the superior British forces. He was court marshalled, and 5 years later the United States was at war again.

Without a superior harbor, or a bigtime name to prop up its fortunes, Port Ludlow never became a major town. It is an extremely affluent town, however, one of the richest in the state, which is surprising due to its humble origins.

SILVERDALE, WA

In 1878, a settler by the name of William Littlewood found his way to what is now called Silverdale. When he platted the land, his original idea was
to name the area "Goldendale" but since that name
was already occupied by a sleepy hamlet in Eastern
Washington, Littlewood's vast creativity went to
work. Silver was just as good, or at least, a very close
second, to gold, and the town named Silverdale was
born. 'Just as good' and 'close second' would be dom-
inant themes throughout Silverdale's days. Over 150
years later, what was once a small logging community
has blossomed into the retail center of the Central
Kitsap Peninsula. If you had to find a defining word
for Silverdale, you can't find a better word than retail.

Home to a sprawling mall complex, hundreds of
cookie cutter stores all boasting frontages similar and
depressingly familiar, and even a Costco, Silverdale
has all the charm and appeal of your average strip
mall. Over the past 30 years, the small town has built
itself into a retail juggernaut, siphoning business
away from the more down-home and local businesses
of its neighbor Bremerton. It wasn't always this way.
It used to be quite cozy--nice, even.

Up until the early 1970's, Silverdale was primarily a farming community that enjoyed a logging and fishing tradition. Early settlers were mostly from Scandinavian stock, quiet and hardworking people, shying away from the raucous and tantalizing orgy that was Bremerton in its early days. Then, the military, as it's wont to do, changed everything. In 1971, the Navy decided to build a submarine base just north of Silverdale and the town's people lost their collective minds. Home prices skyrocketed, new housing developments were built seemingly overnight, and with the influx of people came the stores. Lots and lots of stores. Old landmarks were lost in record time and the small, quiet, and some say "charming" quality of the town was lost forever.

Honestly, this rebranding of small town America into a commercial "paradise" is occurring all over at a rapid pace. Smaller communities have to fight harder than ever to retain even a modicum of their former heritage, most content to keep that history in a tiny trailer called the local historical society. Are older, historical buildings cost effective? No, of course not, but that's not the point. The point is, I've never once found a Walmart or Costco to be charming, or inspiring, much less beautiful. Anything built after 1970 has all the character of a concrete slab, but concrete is cheap and so that's the direction we go. While

I appreciate the economic reasons for the transition, I can't help but feel that we are losing something vital in the transaction.

You can still see a glimpse of the past in the downtown area, though it's more saturated with the new than a remembrance of the old.

ESSAYS FROM THE SOUND

OWNING MINIVANS AND OTHER BAD IDEAS

I'm not sure why vehicles today have to be so plain. Maybe the answer lies somewhere in my old microeconomics textbook, but that offers small comfort as I see yet another neutral-toned tribute to bland design cut me off on the freeway. Not that the car I drive is a revelation or unique, but I always feel a twinge of regret and a certain nostalgia for our automotive days gone by.

I took my family to a car museum once and enjoyed every moment of the experience. The place had a century's worth of makes and models on display in an impressive, metallic, Twinkie-shaped building. Exploring its four floors, I was in awe as we strolled down aisle after aisle of interesting and well-formed cars. You can tell that great thought and passion went into making each one. They all had a character that can't be matched today. I'm not a car guy by any stretch of the imagination, but I felt myself getting rather excited at the sight of so many finely crafted machines.

Not surprisingly, the one car they did not have on display in the museum was a minivan, the epitome of plain and boring car design.

My wife hates minivans more than almost anything. She once told me that there was no circumstance in all the world that could force her to willingly choose to drive a minivan for any length of time. Her view is that all minivans resemble turds with the end pinched off and she'd rather they all be flushed, as is proper procedure with turds. Fair enough.

In my more precocious moods, which are all too often, I decide to test her on this by proposing impossible situations where she would be forced to choose the comfort and safety of a minivan. She has yet to be swayed. Not that I want a minivan, mind you, it's just fun to see how far she will go.

The other day, we zipped past an ocher PT Cruiser. It was the color of sickly urine, that dark yellow color that you get when you're not feeling too well. The PT Cruiser is widely recognized as one of the most unfortunate-looking cars ever built. Widely, that is, except for a small but vocal minority that refuses to accept that they have bad taste.

I proposed the far-flung situation in which she was forced to pick between driving the ocher PT Cruiser or driving any minivan in the world. She turned open-mouthed at me and gave me that hurt and disbelieving look that all wives have, horrified that I would make her choose. The choice in no way represented reality, I wouldn't want to own either type of car, but in that moment I could not reliably tell you that she knew I was kidding. The look on her face was one of betrayal, hurt, and anger, all wrapped up into one.

But mostly anger.

I feared for my life.

That was the last time I mentioned such a thing and our marriage is all the better for it.

PERILS OF RADIO PLAY
AND DYING

As a teenager, I lived in a fantasy world of gangster rap. Not that I was hardcore, or anything other than privileged, lower-middle class white America, but my friend and I felt that Dr. Dre and Snoop Diggity Dogg spoke to us. It was a phase, I suppose.

My friend Robbie and I would go around, not exactly pretending we were 'gangstas,' but quoting and singing these songs. Rob was better at this than me. He had the keener insight into a thug's life since his neighborhood was far more dangerous than mine. The worst thing you'd find on my street was a woman everyone called Grandma who said the word 'bum' as a substitute for 'butt.' Not very gangsta.

We spent most of our early teens learning the words to, but not brave enough to live by, the songs of Dre and Snoop. We rather liked their videos as well, as there was always some bikini-clad woman running around, and that seemed like a good way to live one's life. That may have been the impetus for us liking the music in the first place, but I really can't remember.

Eventually, the lauded partnership between Dr.

Dre and Snoop Doggy Dogg dissolved. Snoop was ready to hit the road by himself and came out with his own album, Doggystyle, a term Rob and I both understood to be dirty but didn't really know why. The album sold a million copies in the first week and the main single from the album, called "What's My Name?" was all over the radio.

Since Rob and I were too young to buy an album with explicit lyrics, we had to settle for bootlegs taped off of the radio. Taping songs off the radio was a little tricky, but we soon became masters and had ourselves some sweet mixtapes. It was my Snoop Dogg mixtape that got me into trouble with my mom.

My mom picked Rob and me up from church youth group one night, and I had our Snoop Dogg mixtape in my pocket. Maybe we just needed a hit of sweet Snoop, but I asked if it was okay if I put our tape in the player. Knowing my music taste differed from hers, Mom was understandably concerned, perhaps even wary, but allowed it to happen. I slid the tape in and Snoop Dogg's voice filled the car singing "What's My Name?"

Frankly, you should never listen to young music with older people, it is not good for anyone's digestion. As Mom listened to the lyrics, her face gradually distorted from confusion to disgust to wonderment that this was being played on the radio.

"And where did you get this?" she asked several times.

"The radio Mom, they couldn't play it if it was bad," I reassured her in my snarky, teenage way. I'm actually surprised I didn't get smacked.

It was at that moment that Snoop said, in the PG-13 radio version of his song, "I'm the 'G' with the biggest sack, and who's that…" Everyone stopped talking and my mom felt compelled to repeat, "The G with the biggest sack? What does that mean?"

Neither Rob nor I felt ready to answer questions about gangster testicles, especially regarding their size or manliness, and certainly not with my mom asking. Undeterred by our silence, my mom persisted, "Do either of you know what that means? G with the biggest sack?" This went on for a full, supremely embarrassing minute before I finally got the hint and removed the tape.

"I should probably think twice before playing these things when you're around."

"Not unless you have the sack to answer my questions," she said. My mom was funny, in hindsight, and I couldn't disagree with her. Shortly thereafter, rap lost its appeal and I really haven't looked back since.

After my brief love affair with rap, I never really bothered listening to radio. For some reason, I prefer my own thoughts and company to any of the nonsense that usually passes for pop music. Of course, then I began listening to public radio and other talk radio stations. I think it's a rule when you age that several things that must take place in rapid succession. First, hair grows in unwanted places, then creaking in the muscles, and finally, you start listening to NPR.

Fifteen years later, on my way to a laundromat, I casually flipped on the radio. My wife, who I suspect will always be hipper and cooler than I (due to her being a whole three weeks younger than me), regularly listens to popular stations. I know that I sound like a curmudgeon, but some of these songs are truly horrible. Since my wife was the last to drive, one of these songs was on the radio as I turned it on.

It was about Sadomasochistic Sex.

A woman singing about brutal sex is quite startling if you aren't expecting it. The lady sang something about "sex in the air," and I will admit that my ears perked a bit. Then she said "but whips and chains excite me," followed by what I can only assume was an overly graphic description of how excited she was by these instruments of torture. I don't know for certain because as soon as I heard the line, I inadvertently exclaimed, "For Pete's Sake!" and my hand shot out, of its own will, to change the station.

I can't be certain which button I pressed, my hand acting of its own accord and all, but whichever one I did, it seemed to be the wrong one. The radio lit up, started blinking, and the stations skipped ahead like a machine possessed. I have this effect on some older electronics. After a minute of losing its mind, the radio decided to choose a station for me, obviously disapproving of the previous song as well. It landed on the soft rock station, you know the type, the feel good channel that does anything but. Try as I might, I could not get the station to change. I was stuck.

That was when Kenny G began to play. I sighed and turned the radio off.

In the case of a fiery car crash, I refused to die to a soundtrack of soft rock music. Kenny G should certainly not be the last thing you hear in this world. I wouldn't wish that on anyone.

THAT TIME MY DAD WORE A SPEEDO

When I was 12 years old, my father managed to embarrass me more than I thought was possible. His tools of torture were some middle-aged bravado, my entire 6th-grade class, and a smallish Speedo. It was a night to remember.

The scene is thus: I attended a private Lutheran school from 5th to 8th grade. One of the highlights was the yearly tournament creatively called Lutheran Elementary School Tournament, or LEST for short. LEST was a pre-pubescent bacchanalia of young men and women battling in such diverse events as knowledge bowls, spelling bees, volleyball, and even basketball. It was our elementary school Olympics, except we got one every year.

Besides the competitions, LEST was a chance for heady teenage hormones to go a little wild. More than 15 schools stayed in the same hotels, so it was an excellent opportunity to find young people of the opposite sex and stare at them awkwardly. At least, that was my custom in those days. Often, the best place to find a large cluster of young people was the pool area. This was why, two nights into the event, my friend Robbie and I were champing at the bit to go down to the pool. It was about as close to James Bond strolling into a Montenegro Casino and seducing a foreign beauty as we were likely to get at that age.

We were primed with our swimsuits and towels, feeling pretty confident in ourselves, when my Mom delivered the terrible news.

"Oh, boys! Wait up, your Dad and sisters are coming with you," she said.

To a 12-year-old hoping to catch the notice of and perhaps, maybe, talk to a pretty girl from another school, this was the kiss of death. Invariably, I would be put in charge of my sister's safety and my great plans of lust and love would never bear fruit. We slumped on the bed and in unison let out a deep lip-sputtering sigh.

My sisters changed in the other room and my father went to the bathroom. The girls were surprisingly swift, re-entering our room with shrill and excited laughter, but my Dad was taking his time. One thing I learned early in life: there's no hurrying my father in the bathroom. So we waited.

The bathroom door swung open and my father emerged with what I can only describe as a flourish. There he was, barely covered in the smallest bathing suit I have ever had the misfortune of seeing. It was a tiny black thread of a thing, with enough fabric around the groin to be considered, technically, legal. It left little to the imagination.

"Oh, Craig! No!" My mother rightly exclaimed.

"What?" my father said, attempting to look sincerely befuddled.

"You cannot wear that to the pool," my mother said. Her face betrayed the anguish that the man she had pledged to love was capable of such bad decision-making.

"We agree with Mom!" the kids all said in unison, even my friend, who had ridden with us and didn't have another ride home.

My father waved us off. "It's fine, it covers everything."

No one said a word, we just continued to stare uncomfortably.

"Fine, I'll put on a robe until we get down there and slip into the pool so no one will see. This is the only suit I brought." He said this as if that made the whole matter clear and digestible.

He quickly grabbed a robe, threw it on, and motioned us toward the door. "Come on, the pool awaits." Just minutes before, those words that held so much promise filled me with a terminal dread.

We walked down the hallway to the elevator and rode down in silence. No one wanted to acknowledge the situation. I prayed that this was the one time of day that no one from my school, or any school, would be at the pool. The doors opened and we walked out of the elevator directly into the pool area.

God was not my friend that day and my prayers were not answered. It seemed that Robbie and I had missed a memo because my entire class was in the pool area, splashing around and generally carrying on like 12-year-olds do. Only a few kids noticed us, waving their hellos as they dived back into the mass of arms and legs.

Robbie and I quickly found places for our towels and dived into the pool. My sisters did the same. Dad had a different agenda. With uncharacteristic enthusiasm and showmanship, he whipped off his robe and tossed it towards our towels, exposing himself to everyone. Robbie and I discovered that looking up at my Dad in a Speedo was worse than looking down.

I don't know if it was his intention but all activity in the pool ceased. Not a word whispered, not a ripple was made. All eyes were now on my Dad and his barely-there European-style bathing suit. A young man swam up behind me--Rick, the class jerk, the one everyone hates but follows anyway--and said, "Hey, isn't that your Dad?"

"I, uh, uh," I responded. Most twelve-year-old boys are not equipped to handle complex social situations like these and I was no exception.

"Dork," Rick said as he splashed the side of my face. With that humiliation, some life came back as everyone shifted their attention from my father's package to their previous activities. Though, their attentions were divided with constant glances back to make sure my Dad held his place.

In response to the extra attention, my father decided to do possibly the worst thing a middle-aged man wearing a tiny bathing suit around almost-teenagers could do; he stretched. Arms spread, he arched his back and had a good long stretch. I looked up, mouth hung open at his audacity. Then I noticed the looks on the faces of the moms lounging around the pool. It was a mixture of admiration and horror. He then dived into the water and started playing a pool game with my sisters, as if everything was normal.

Over the next twenty minutes, these quietly appreciative Lutheran mothers led their children away from the pool area. They each left with a parting glance at my Dad and I knew that we were the reason they hastened their exit. Eventually, we were the only ones left in the pool.

I was thoroughly embarrassed and I don't recall ever being angrier with my Dad. It seemed like the most selfish thing I had ever seen him do, which hurt more since he was supposed to be at the event for our sake. At least, that's how I saw it then. More than twenty years later, I think I understand things a little better.

At the time, my father was 36 years old and had been working out steadily for over a year. He was struggling to overcome the dreaded middle age flabby look that many of his friends had succumbed to and he succeeded in fighting back admirably. So at 36, with the toned body of a teenager, my Dad just wanted to show off a little. Now, why he chose to display his new physique to a group of prepubescent teenagers and their parents is a question I may never have answered, but as an older man in my thirties, looking down at a larger belly than I'd like, I think I understand my Dad a little better.

FREE CHEESE FROM
A DIRTY BIN

After a long and happy anniversary weekend, my wife and I decided to cap off the experience with a trip to the Tillamook Cheese Factory. While I'm a fan of things that don't require money to leave my pocket, I was not sure of this trip. Tillamook Cheese is middling at best - nothing fancy - it's a higher level of cheese for the masses. If you're at the grocery store, and you want to show that you are fancier than everyone at the party, or you live in a housing development called Devonshire Landing, you buy Tillamook instead of the store brand. The label makes it tastes better.

My wife is a fan of cheese as a rule (due to her French heritage, I suppose), so Tillamook cheese, straight from the cheese factory, was too good to pass up. Did I mention it was free? We had to go.

We hopped on highway 101 and headed north. The road weaved along, as most small coastal highways do, dipping in and out of small towns, promising a robust cruising speed of 55 MPH but instantly disappointing with a cautionary sign telling you to slow to 40 at the next curve. There was always a next curve. The drive was pleasant enough, but we were both eager to reach our destination after hours of driving; my wife for cheese and myself for other, more lavatorial reasons.

The town of Tillamook comes on suddenly, then lingers uncertainly, like a creepy uncle who loses his nerve. We passed through the town, confused about where they put the factory. Minutes passed as we drove along the highway that passed as the main road through town. We both got that feeling you get when you think you've missed your destination, and that you should turn around, but you have no concrete evidence to support your theory.

We even passed a large barn promising fancy French cheeses and wine tastings, a most friendly union and certainly a pairing Tillamook did not offer, but we were set in our mission. We were going to a real cheese factory.

Shortly after we passed the cheese barn, and mere moments away from turning around because I was convinced we made a serious error in direction, we saw the sign for the cheese factory showroom. Rather, I saw the massive factory in the distance, occupying more space than several airplane hangars, and then the large yellow sign. It was huge and unsettling.

"Oh, there it is! Cheese, cheese, cheese," my wife began to chant. Her high spirits rubbed off and I began to think that maybe this free cheese excursion could actually be fun. I sang along in the spirit of the moment.

We turned into the Tillamook Cheese Factory parking lot, which had a surface area that rivaled the largest of Walmarts. The sheer scope of the operation was unbelievable. Even worse, cars filled every inch of the lot. Hoards of people streamed in and out of the building, blank stares carried on fast-shifting, purposeful legs. I looked over at my wife and gave her a smile, the best I could muster, "This should be fun." I said.

She smiled back, but I could tell her enthusiasm had diminished at the sight of so many tourists. This was not what she imagined.

After several minutes and some robust maneuvering on my part, we were lucky enough to find a spot. A white SUV sped away as we parked, the father driving had a clenched face and look of grave determination as his kids screamed in the back seat. I knew his pain, but could do nothing but say a silent prayer. We made our way across the parking lot and toward the cheese factory entrance.

My first thought was that the entrance looked remarkably like a grocery store, complete with large glass panes set in brown steel and automatic sliding doors. They were the kind I used to unhelpfully step in front of when I was a kid and tell people, "After you." We walked around a group of shabbily dressed tourists standing in the middle of the doorway and proceeded inside. Our spirits fell almost immediately.

Whoever designed the Tillamook Cheese Factory showroom had the unique and unerring knack for designing an experience totally devoid of sense or joy. Aside from taking all the worst aspects of fast food restaurants and grocery stores, then mixing those with a seedy carnival atmosphere, there was simply nothing fun about the place. We strolled through the crowds, hoping to find some kind of redemption, mouths agape at the spectacle before us.

The entire facility was dedicated to selling Tillamook cheeses and ice cream. That's fine, I suppose, but the factory was selling the exact same products you could buy at the Fred Meyer grocery store down the street. And they were unfathomably more expensive at the factory. At least you got to wait in a long line for the privilege of paying more. I saw a man happily place two half gallons of ice cream at a register, complete with a conveyor belt just like the grocery store, and nearly lost my mind. The only thing keeping me from walking out was the promise of free cheese and the knowledge that my wife was excited about that idea.

We found the free cheeses in the back of the

showroom. There was an island set up with plastic bins on each side, like a salad bar. In the bins were samples of Tillamook's block cheeses, cut into small cubes, and strict instructions for patrons to take only one piece of cheese per bin. My wife and I watched as small grubby hands joined large grubby hands, plucking chunks of cheese and plopping them into waiting mouths, only to move on to the next series of bins and repeat the process. I tried to estimate how much saliva was deposited on the cheeses in the final bin. It could not have been a small amount.

The worst part was the line for these free cheeses, which were nothing luxurious or interesting--mild cheddar anyone?--stretched around the corner. We would have had to wait in a loud and obnoxious line to eat plain, store bought, saliva-coated cheese. But it was free and what my wife wanted, and, her happiness being my mission, I said nothing and soldiered on.

She leaned over at that moment and said something to me that I will never forget and always cherish to our last day. She leaned into me and said, "I think we've made a huge mistake." No six words and a contraction have given me quite as much joy and my response was an immediate, "Let's go."

"There's that cheese barn down the street," she commented.

"Perfect," I said.

We high-tailed it back to our car. As we neared our spot, that same white SUV with the patience-challenged father drove by us. The father, seeing our intent, slowed down but quickly changed his mind as the car behind him honked. He swore and drove on. I thought about warning him of the dreadful situation awaiting him but quickly thought better of it. Nothing good comes when you try to impose your morals on another. Better for him to decide for himself.

We drove out of the parking lot and both felt that we dodged a bullet, or, at least, some disgusting cheese and an extra disease or two. The cheese barn down the street, though it lacked the polish of Tillamook, was lovely and felt like we were visiting a beloved Aunt's house.

We had a grand time. They even had free cheese samples and served Tillamook ice cream in waffle cones. Really, what more could you want?

STRUGGLES WITH LAUNDRY[1]

Your typical laundromat has all the appeal of dumpster diving, but without the neat surprises. I have always been fascinated by a place that has machines capable of handling of 62 pounds of laundry at a time. If 62 lbs of laundry seems like a lot, that's because it's the same weight as a small, angry child.

Of course, that's good news for me since I hate doing laundry and save up clothes for at least two, sometimes three weeks. The pile of clothes grows unmanageable and I realize that I have been wear-

---

1   The original version of this story was lost to the digital wasteland--I forgot to save--where I can only hope that it has found a happy and fulfilling life, with a wife and family, maybe a house in the country with a dog and a willing audience that it can tell itself to. I wish it all the best. Since I will never see it again, I automatically assume it's superior to this version and if you don't like this version, you can assume that there is a much better and far more engaging version somewhere, living a happy and successful life. For those with too much time on their hands, or the chronically insane, you can search for this lost version, but I don't hold much hope. I doubt it wants to be found since the expectation would be staggeringly unfair to live up to. I don't blame it for staying away, that is, even if it could come back.

ing the same pair of underwear for an undetermined amount of time. At that point, it's time to pack up the car and do some laundry.

Every time I pulled up to the laundromat, I had to remind myself that I am not a loser. There's something about being in your 30s and not owning a washer that brings shame to my American blood. It seems wrong somehow. I reminded myself that we actually had hookups for a washer and dryer in our place. We also have three cats and the only place the cat litter boxes could fit was under the washer/dryer hookups. It was either doing laundry at home and keeping the litter boxes in the kitchen or I go to the laundromat. Sacrifices must be made. As they often do, the cats won out.

I stumbled into the laundromat carrying 800lbs of unsteady laundry as it threatened to become better acquainted with the floor at every step. I reached the door, I discovered it was a pull, not a push. Of course.

I clumsily entered and an unnecessarily cheerful woman greeted me, asking if I had been there before. When I told her that I had not, her unnatural smile grew wider, but not unpleasantly so. She lithely snatched my baskets away from my strained arms. Properly humbled by a woman old enough to have invented the practice of laundry to begin with, I simply hung my head and followed her toward the machines.

With my eyes averted, I noticed the floor gleamed, shined even, something no one expects to see when they visit a laundromat. Then the smell hit me. It was a pleasant and wonderful aroma; fresh laundry. It occurred to me that every laundromat should smell like this on principle.

Most laundry facilities are not inviting. Ironic that establishments designed for cleaning never receive a similar treatment. Which leads to the laundromat smell. Often it's an unwholesome combination of old wet dog, molded soap, and what I can only assume is the smell of dead body, possibly coming from the walls, a successful suicide by someone forced to use a laundromat's often infuriatingly substandard washing machines. This new laundromat seemed to suffer from none of these deficiencies.

The woman marched to a washing machine that looked perfectly capable of handling a car-sized load and threw my clothes into the washing container bin thingy. It's a technical term. To my horror, as she stuffed my clothes into the container bin thingy, a pair of my dirty underwear fell to the ground, right in front of her feet.

Alas, these were not your average male soiled unmentionables, with one or two streaks that can be easily explained. No, this pair was in such a state as to make strangers question whether I should be in public without supervision or, at least, a diaper[2]. To her credit, the woman made no mention of my underwear and swept the garment off the floor, plopping it into the container bin thingy. She abruptly pointed to the laundry detergent, then held out her hand.

Wordlessly I handed her my detergent, amazed at both her efficiency and bravery. Not just anyone would swipe a stranger's underwear off the ground without complaining. This was obviously a woman who had seen a thing or two in her day.

The woman measured out a precise amount of soap, poured it into the appropriate receptacle on the washer, then pointed aggressively to the coin slot. I placed my coins in the slot without hesitation, since her silent movements were becoming more violent. I placed the exact amount of quarters in the slot and moved back. With a small amount of ceremony, the woman gently pressed the start button, then took a step back, staring intently at the machine. I stared intently as well, glancing at her to make sure I was doing it right.

When she was certain that all was well, the woman gave a firm head nod in the direction of the machine, then turned to me, and gave me the same

---

2   Please... don't ask.

nod. I did my best to imitate the motion. She plod-ded to the main office and stayed there.

I washed and dried my pile of clothes in record time. As I was stumbling out the door with my clean load, I popped my head into the office to say my goodbyes. The office was lit a dim bluish glow. The woman sat reclined in her chair, feet propped on a folding table, working an overused toothpick deeper into her gums and staring at the wall. I gave the cus-tomary "I'm going now, thank you so much for your help" head nod. She nodded solemnly in my direc-tion, in the same manner of a cowboy addressing the kid that almost got him killed six or seven times. She went back to contemplating the wall. Instead of being insulted or dismayed, I felt heartened by this, like she had more important things to think about besides my impending leave.

She was wonderful and not a word was exchanged between us beyond the initial question, for which I found myself grateful. At other laundries, random patrons feel the need to engage in lengthy conversa-tions about the minutia of their lives to anyone sta-tionary (and polite) enough to listen. Sometimes the conversations continue without your presence as you go change out your laundry to the dryer, and when you return you find that not much was said in your absence.

Thankfully, my new laundromat offered only the best and I prayed that it would never leave me. I might even start to enjoy doing the laundry.

SUPERMARKET WOES

I dislike retail stores. First, and perhaps foremost, they make me part with my money. My father instilled in me a deep and lasting cheapness, which he called "being thrifty," so my blood boils at the thought of handing over any sum larger than the pleasant clinks of coins. Another reason is having to interact with and be civil to the kind of people who, when they cut you off on the road, feel it justified to give you the bird. Add to that the fluorescent lights, the ill-conceived parking lots, stale air, bad service, rude pedestrians who stroll in front of your car, and that unyielding feeling that you are forgetting something (which inevitably proves to be so, regardless of how well you planned your list), shopping is a less-than-ideal experience.

In short, I hate shopping, but sometimes you have to go.

One crisp fall afternoon I was on my way to the supermarket because I'm the most wonderful husband in the entire world, or so my wife tells me. She was under the weather and I valiantly offered to run her errands. It's not that I never did the shopping, but I hate supermarkets and she has a natural talent for knowing where everything is in any grocery store we visit. She's amazing.

Before stepping foot in the grocery store, I enjoyed a secretive meal from Burger King. Fast food gives me a guilty mixture of hedonistic pleasure and rational regret. It's the pain of knowing that in only a few hours, the tasty food will exact a heavy price, intestinally speaking.

I pulled into the supermarket parking lot and desperately hoped that my inevitable fast-food-induced intestinal hurricane would wait until I finished shopping. I did not want to use the bathroom in the store. Supermarket bathrooms, being open to the public at all hours, are not known for their superior cleanliness. When you visit a supermarket bathroom, you don't bother to wash your hands when you finish up--what's the point? Rather, you head straight for the cleaning aisle and pour close to a gallon of hand sanitizer over yourself. It's the only way to go.

I absentmindedly walked into the grocery store, as is my custom. Too often, I find more important things to do with my time than pay attention to where I am walking. This habit often leads me to small disasters and this time was no different. I entered the store where I assumed the exit should have been. Unfortunately, the store was not obeying the common rules of the road and decided to switch things up. In

America, we drive on the right and naturally expect the entrance and exit door we use to follow our national policy. This store decided to spurn tradition and reverse it, for no reason that I could see other than to screw with the customers. An exiting mother with 14 children parading around her cart like young heathens demanding a sacrifice almost crashed into me. Her look turned from startled, to angry, to loathing as I impeded her exit. I tried to give her an apologetic look, but the damage was done.

I walked toward the aisles and saw that each item on my list was sectioned out into groups. Knowing her, my wife listed every item according to its aisle in the store. Unfortunately, knowing which aisle to start with presented a problem. I went right, with the nagging feeling that I should have gone left, and after a minute of wandering, ended up doing just that. I detest every single minute of my grocery adventures.

Random Quick Tip: Never settle for anything called 'Value Cheese' from the bargain bins. Yes, it's cheap, but any positive expectations of the product are sure to be dashed immediately upon its entering the mouth.

My shopping at a supermarket is mostly an exercise in wandering. Stock boys and cashiers see me pass by several times in the course of a few minutes and try to keep their distance as I mutter to myself.

The truth is, I can never remember where anything is, and the large signs provided above every aisle are only of limited help. The signs only show the broadest of categories anyway, and invariably the thing that I need is not listed publicly. While my wife can memorize the entire schematic of the store in a single visit, I am lucky to find the produce section in under 5 minutes, even after I've been there before.

On my way out of the produce section, I passed the wine aisle. There was a young man there with his girlfriend or wife, it's hard to tell these days. I heard this young man attempt to impress his girlfriend by mentioning that "2010" was a good vintage for a certain bottle of wine because it's been resting for 5 years. The young lady was impressed by his vast knowledge and cooed appropriately. The bottle of wine in question was $3. A little tip for those that don't know, there is no good vintage for a $3 bottle of wine. It serves one purpose and taste is not it.

Unfortunately, this is when the fast food decided to make its presence felt. My guts twisted in horrifying knots as warning bells in my head urged me to find a bathroom quickly. By some holy miracle, I saw the restroom sign and headed in that direction.

Once I reached the bathroom, the door was locked and room occupied. I waited, keeping perfectly still in the way people do when they are trying to avoid soiling themselves. To distract myself from impending doom, I looked around at the posters on the wall.

They had everything from your standard employee warning posters written in print so tiny that no one would actually take the time to find a magnifying glass powerful enough to decipher the words, to flyers announcing that people need to pick up after themselves in the break room. The most disturbing poster was plastered against the door to the cooler. It was a poster detailing the process of recycling the store's meat. The meat recycling process involves a rubber bin, several trash bags, and a magic wand. At least, that's what I presume because I didn't get a chance to finish reading. The bathroom door opened and I went in.

It's impossible to fully describe the stench that accumulates in a store bathroom, especially one that has been in operation for years. The smell seems to ooze out of the walls. It touches your skin like an unwanted predator. Every surface has a dull, matte finish from years of polishing and cleaning. Everything is dingy. The woman who exited before me had her head down, I then recalled, and as I peered into the unflushed toilet I saw why. I did my business as quickly as possible and left to find the sanitizer.

I finished up my shopping, paid for the groceries, left my cart in the front of the store, and picked my items. A lady came up, obviously in need of a grocery cart, so I politely motioned to the one I just finished using. Instead of a hearty and sincere thank you for saving her the time and trouble of finding her own cart, she proceeded to give me a thorough once-over. First up, then down. And not in a flattering way. Then she looked at the cart, carefully took out an industrial-sized hand sanitizer from her purse, and wiped down the entire handle. I just stood and watched, not saying a word, as she finished cleaning my filth from her now shiny cart and wheeled off into the store. I figured she could somehow sense that I used the store's bathroom.

My journey to grocery stores is never complete without being accosted in the parking lot, mostly by folks just looking for a dollar or two because they suddenly ran out of gas. This time, a man approached me for the following conversation;

"Did you see that weird guy around here?"

"No," I told him, "can't say that I have."

"Well, I told him to go f&$k off, he's weird."

With that, the man walked away, twitching slightly.

Did I mention I hate shopping?

THE TYRANNY OF
1980S CARTOONS

The other day, as I watched my wife's cat leap across the furniture, I had a childhood flashback. His cat body flying through the air reminded me of a beloved cartoon called Voltron, Defender of the Universe.

If you're not old enough to know, Voltron was an exceptionally popular cartoon in the eighties. It was about a band of intrepid space explorers who traveled to a planet, awakened an ancient defense system comprised of five lion robots, and combined those lions to form a super robot named Voltron. I think I'm making it sound better than it really was.

The real promise of the cartoon, as with most cartoons from the 1980s, was actually in the merchandise. Brainwashed by the 20 minutes of commercials for toys in my 30-minute show, I desperately wanted to own the five lions so I could defend the universe with my very own Voltron.

Unfortunately, every other kid in the entire world wanted a Voltron set at the same time. Because of economics or something, that made the cost prohibitive, about a million dollars. In any case, the price was much too high for my parents.

Thriftiness leads to heartbreaks, especially for a young boy, but it also forces one to be creative. Instead of mortgaging their house to buy me a toy that would give me, at most, a month of splendid happiness, they made a deal with me that I was sure to lose.

I was five when Voltron took hold of me, leaving me functionally unable to think about anything else. I also had a terrible bed wetting problem. I can admit this now that I don't often do it. At the time, though, it was a real headache for everyone involved. Me, because I had to sleep in urine and my parents because they were tired of cleaning up bodily fluids. My father, in one of his fits of enterprise, saw an opportunity. He promised me that if I didn't wet the bed for 30 days, they would buy me a Voltron set, all five lions. My excitement was palpable.

I went to bed that night, determined that no urine would escape my body without expressed consent. I was the master of my destiny and my pee.

I awoke that night to a wet, cold lake under my stomach. Dejected, I pulled myself from the soggy mattress and trudged into my parents room. Soiled pajamas in hand, I woke up my Dad with the smell of a 5-year old's pee-soaked pajama bottoms. For parents, this is not a completely unexpected way to wake up, but certainly not a welcome one, especially not on a Saturday morning. Bleary eyed, he looked at me, looked at my bottoms, and assessed the situation.

"Tough break kiddo," he said.

"Yeah," I barely responded, the tears flowed freely as I imagined my beautiful plastic lions leaping away from me into the horizon.

'Too bad you can't control your whiz,' said the yellow lion as he lagged behind the others just so he could give me a crappy look. I never liked the yellow one.

"I guess you'll just have to start over," my Dad said and laid back down. It was early, maybe 4am, so when I look back now, I'm grateful for the lucidity my father showed that early in the morning.

At the prospect of owning my beloved toy, and knowing that the chase was not yet done, I impulsively hugged my Dad and said, "Thank you thank you thank you!" I ran out of the room to grab some towels for the bed. In my head, the lions came roaring back over the horizon, full of promise and hope. The yellow lion was silently glum.

I grabbed my bowl of cereal from the kitchen and turned on the TV, waiting for Saturday morning cartoons like every other kid in America. Despite my failure, I had an odd sensation that anything was possible. Sure, I messed my bed again, but I had a chance to do something great that no else had ever done in the history of kiddom. Win Voltron.

I was determined to make this happen, no matter what. This time, the lions would be mine and nothing would get in my way. That night I prayed with my Dad the most selfish prayer any child has ever uttered, entreating God for his grace and hand upon my bladder.

"Lord," I said, "Please don't let me pee the bed so that Dad will have to buy me a Voltron. Amen." That was it, the sum of my being and everything I wanted in life up to that point. To stop urinating and win my Voltron. Nothing else mattered.

That night I didn't pee the bed. It was the first time in a long time, months I suppose, and I woke up clean and dry. It was a miraculous way to greet the day and I jumped out of bed with a dance in my step. I, of course, went immediately to my parent's room to wake them up.

"Dad! I didn't wet the bed!"

"Good job kiddo," he said, obviously annoyed that I woke him up two days in a row, at a time people shouldn't be awake on the weekends. "Only 29 days left to go."

At the time, I took this as an affirmation that he was proud of me and rooting for me to win. I'm sure he was glad that I didn't wet the bed, that I didn't have to sleep in my pee, and that he didn't have to wash my sheets again, but I'm not sure it was pride. And he wasn't rooting for me to win.

I know this because making a deal with anyone based on controlling uncontrollable bodily reflexes doesn't make sense. It's like when someone who knows biology better than you do makes a bet that they can make you blink. Not knowing any better, you take that bet, steeling yourself for any and every onslaught they could possibly throw at you. Then they do something so simple that, even at a young age, it seems like it should have occurred to you. They blow in your face. You blink uncontrollably. They win the bet. It's an unfair bet, every kid who has done it or been tricked by it knows this. I'm sure I knew it too when my Dad made the deal with me but, you know, Voltron.

I actually went a whole week without waking up moist and was starting to believe that God had answered my prayer. He had given me mastery over my developing bladder. Then Monday morning, it happened: a wet pool of urine soaked through into my mattress once again. It was as if my body had somehow made up for lost time and released the floodgates. I came and got my Dad, tears in my eyes to show him my disappointment. He helped me clean up and three towels later, the mattress was only a little damp.

"Do I have to start over?" I asked, terror and hope mingling together in my face.

"I'm sorry son, a deal's a deal. You have to go thirty days without wetting the bed, then we'll buy you a Voltron."

It was a heartbreaking declaration. I couldn't fathom how to control my bladder, and I did not. True to my father's secret hopes, I never made it thirty days without wetting the bed. I mean, I did eventually (my wife is very thankful my body learned to keep the pee inside and not on her), but by the time I acquired that skill, I had moved on to other toys and hobbies.

Later that year, after I had become the full master of my whiz--take that, yellow lion--my parents must have felt a pang of guilt for crushing the dreams and hopes of their only son. I came home from school to find a present in my room, a bin of Legos, my favorite.

They bought the large generic tub, the one with a thousand pieces of various colors and sizes, but all brickish in nature. These were the glory days before the fancy sets where all the work is done for you. There were no elegant plastic recreations of your favorite cartoons or TV shows; you had to supply those yourself. It was no Voltron, but I eventually got over that, as kids do.

I think I was better off with the generic tub of bricks in the end. The tub opened me up to think creatively and make the world bend to my will rather than be a slave to the imaginations and, frankly, the bad storytelling of Hasbro and their ilk. I was free to tell my own bad stories and revel in them for hours.

Still, it would have been pretty sweet to play with those lions, even for just a little while.

CATS, BATHROOMS, AND MASSAGING MAN PARTS

One beautiful Saturday morning, I woke with a terrible case of the grumps and no motivation to move. I barely summoned the energy necessary to nudge my wife to wake up as well. If I had to get up and face the day with all of its duties and tasks, I needed my partner with me. She didn't move. I tried again, with the same result.

I sat up, rubbed my eyes, and only then noticed one of our cats kneading me in that way that cats do when they test your body for weakness. Unfortunately, the cat was massaging my man parts. This was not the first time the cat had attempted to get up close and personal with my most sensitive areas, nor would it be the last.

This time, though, he stared into my eyes as he kneaded me.

While I've become accustomed to the near-constant staring behavior of cats, when the cat massages between my legs and stares at me, things take a different turn.

"Tibby NO!" I overreacted and hurled the cat off of our bed. My subtle nudge had no effect on my dear wife, but hearing the cat's screech as I threw him across the room did the trick.

She bolted awake from bed. "What happened?" she asked.

I explained her cat's crotch massage and she chuckled slightly. I won't say that she was delighted, but there's a small gleam of joy she gets in her eyes when one of her cats misbehaves in some small way. It's endearing. She is quite willing to tolerate our beasts in a way that I don't know how. She laid back down and promptly fell back asleep.

I've never desired to be a cat person, but unfortunately, I believe that is what my wife wishes me to become.

She's not openly anti-dog. We had a fine pair of Beagles for a time, but their constant crotch licking did not endear them to her. So, we have cats. One is smaller and cuddly, the other is heavy and always demanding of my attention. Our cats suffer from many of the mysterious behaviors that plague feline psyches, but one stands in my mind as unique to our brood.

A love-hate relationship with the bathroom.

Our cats decided long ago, perhaps in a secret meeting, that the bathroom is the place to be, especially when people are there. However, they aren't entirely sold on the practice. What I mean is that they are of two minds about the whole situation. On one side, they must honor the agreement they obviously set forward to enter the bathroom or demand to be inside with a constant and heartbreaking cry whenever humans choose to use the room. On the other hand, or paw, they despise being trapped inside. Yet, when you open the door they refuse to leave.

Closing the door does nothing to solve this bothersome contradiction for them, in that they will jump on the counter, and headbutt the door handle, a clear indication to any sane individual that the animal would like to leave immediately.

Alas, this could not be farther from the truth.

When you open the door to let him out, removing the door knob from the range of its noggin, the cat will sit on its haunches and look at you with bewilderment. It's as if you have just done the single most idiotic thing a person could do. Cats are singularly gifted with this look, and I believe, though I have no direct evidence to support such a claim, that they practice these despising looks at night. This also explains why they sleep all throughout the day.

There can be no other explanation to my mind.

After another mocking look, withering me to the core most effectively, I close the door again, only to watch the headbutting resume in a manner that suggests, once again, that they wish to be let out. I choose not to fall for the now obvious ruse but my penalty is to watch the cat deform its head on the door. Since I know a cat with a massive dent in its head would upset my wife, I quickly finish what I'm doing and leave the room.

This frees the cat from its previously agreed-upon bondage and all is harmonious in the house once again. Whether it's part of the cats' devious ultimate plan or just a natural consequence of close quarters, I have to say that, despite the sudden bouts of insanity, these furry creatures grow on me. One day, I might even be called a cat person.

God forbid.

THE FALSE NAMER OF THINGS

One sunny day, my work got to be too stressful so I took a walk during my lunch. As a marketing writer, it's my job to make up things that "aren't" to apply to things that "are." Some people call this lying, but I like to think of it as creative truth telling. Yeah, I don't always believe it either.

Just around the block from work, I walked past one of those apartment complexes that you see every day but don't take much notice. It looked like a place people end up, not a place people choose to live. The sides of the buildings were weather-stained and the windows were old, single-pane aluminum, the ones that were only useful for collecting mold spores, not for keeping the cold air out. I'd driven by this complex many times on my way to the office, but it never occurred to me to pay attention until I saw the name.

Alpine Vistas.

Horsehockey, I thought.

Whoever has the job of naming apartment complexes must be an exceedingly happy individual. Morally bankrupt for sure, but proud of himself for scoring such a position. His day consists mainly of taking some mildly pleasant-sounding words like Meadow, Glen, Grove, Creek, Pine, or Alpine and mixing them all together. The one hard-and-fast rule to which this intrepid Namer of Apartments must adhere is this: no matter what, the name must never represent the thing being named, not even a little. In short, you have to be an enthusiastic champion of lying.

The Alpine Vistas Apartments were thousands of miles away from anything remotely considered "alpine." Unless 'alpine' means "parking lot" in some obscure language. My all-time favorite absurd apartment name is Vista View Apartments. Literally it means "View View" which I find doubly pretentious since they are often located across the street from the city dump.

Score a big one for the Namer.

DISTRUST OF NEIGHBORS

As I pulled out of my driveway one day, I saw my neighbor taking out his trash. Instead of waving immediately, like any good neighbor would, my mind jumped into a dark and distrustful place.

I wondered if he had bodies in the garbage bag.

This is terrible, but true. It's not just me, though. I've noticed that most Americans seem to take for granted that everyone is trying to kill us.

Perhaps this is nothing new, but it shows in our conversations, or lack thereof, with our neighbors. How much do people, especially those living in the city, know their neighbors? Not especially well, I think.

Maybe it's because we don't need to, being loosed from the constraints of proximity thanks to the internet. But I think it's more than that. It comes down to the fact that we simply don't trust people.

We look at strangers as potential thieves and murders and not as potential new friends. As if their sole purpose in life is to get chummy with us so they can steal our $35 DVD player or study our habits so that they can better slaughter us in our sleep.

Now, I know that there are other reasons for not making friends with neighbors. Renters don't want to make friends they might have to lose if they move. Perhaps you have a full social calendar (Who needs more friends--Facebook has given me plenty!). Or, you might be utterly disagreeable to everyone you meet, in which case none of this applies to you.

But for those who are generally well-liked, what's your excuse for not getting to know all of your neighbors? Why hide away in a perpetual fog of fear and uncertainty? Are your neighbors really going to kill you? If your answer is "Yes!" to the last question, my advice is to move. I'm fairly certain there exists a community closeby that has diminished degree of murderous intent.

If your excuse for not knowing your neighbors starts with "But..." or "Well...," I would advise that you throw the excuses in the trash. And while you're outside, get to know your neighbors. You never know, you might get a good DVD player out of it.

YOU DEFINITELY SHOULD NOT EAT YOUR KIDS

I'll begin this tale with a well-deserved compliment. My wife happens to be the most patient woman on the planet. I know this because she has decided not to eat our child. Let me explain.

If you watch the good animal documentaries, you might see a mother animal suddenly become tired of her youth's antics and eat him whole. You might assume that this is simply nature taking its course and that animals are too juvenile in their thinking to recognize that eating children goes against the best interest of the species. Anyone who thinks this does not have children who are able to speak.

One day, my wife nearly ended her eleven-year streak of caring for and not consuming our only child. I opened our bedroom door to find our son camped outside our room, vibrating with unknown excitement.

To be so exuberant so early in the day is a young man's game, typically reserved for special occasions like birthdays, Christmas, and the occasional trip to Disneyland. You might add summer break to that list, but not a Saturday morning in March. Washington

State is not known for its glorious March weather, instead saving every possible sunny day for August and September. March is exclusively a wet and cold month where we live.

"What's so exciting?" I asked him, a tinge of grump in my voice that he either ignored or could not hear, due to his vibrations.

He was shaking up and down so hard now the floor sympathized and vibrated along with him, "I made the cat do a backflip!" he said with such pure joy that I couldn't help but laugh. My wife did not find this news nearly as amusing.

She leveled a steely gaze in his direction and asked, "When?" The words drew out in a manner that I immediately recognized as the human equivalent of the lioness growl. I feared for our child.

He was ignorant of her tones, "Right before I put him in your room. Why?"

"Don't do it again," my wife said succinctly, with an impressive amount of self-control.

"Why?" my son asked, not unreasonably, but clearly he was in danger, so I stepped in, "It's not a good idea buddy, okay?"

"But why?" he asked, getting more impatient, "It doesn't hurt him."

My wife sank down to his level, "Because we said so, that's why. Now don't do it again."

My son made a poor decision: "That's dumb, he likes it when I flip him!"

To be fair, our son is not like this, but every once in awhile, his spirited Irish nature gets the best of him. My wife was in no mood for his lip, but there was something else in her demeanor. Her face had that same look a lioness gets when a cub displeases her and is marked for execution. I had to intervene for the safety of our son. "Go to your room right now!" I yelled a little too loud.

As he huffed and slammed his door I added, "And don't come out until you are ready to apologize to your mom."

I looked over at my wife and she ran her hands over her face and said, "I definitely need more sleep." She proceeded into the bathroom. I was left in the hallway, awaiting my turn, but feeling rather happy with myself for averting the inevitable disaster.

HUMAN RESOURCES
AND THE TALIBAN

To the Employees of Taliban Region 2,
From Director of Human Resources McSimmons:

When our mighty rulers first brought me in to deal with personnel "issues" in this once-great division of the Taliban, I was excited to rise up to the challenge. Leaving my former position as the Human Resource Coordinator for Harvey Smithfieldson Furniture in beautiful Gig Harbor, WA, I felt more than prepared for this new and exciting challenge.

After increasing efficiency by 17.2% in my first three weeks (Go, Team!), I admit that I felt that this was the best decision I had ever made. But, after the recent squabbles over office supplies, I am beginning to have my doubts about the morale in this office.

First of all, I know from personal experience how frustrating it is when you feel like you are the only one to replace anything in office. Changing the jug for the water cooler, the paper in the copier, or even toilet paper in the bathroom, the tragedy of the commons weighs heavy on our shoulders. In my past life at Harvey Smithfieldson Furniture, I stood alone in caring whether everyone had adequate supplies to do their work. In that sense, I understand why events transpired the way they did, leading to the tragedies that befell us all.

Because I'm still having trouble saying or even spelling any of your names, I must refer to the two chief antagonists in this sordid tale as Larry and Dan. Those are names I'm more comfortable with, and you know who you are, anyway. From what I gathered, the ruckus began because Larry was zealous in his neatly stacking the small arms in the approved zones. But Larry was matched by Dan's outright defiance, and sabotaging of, the pre-approved small arms stacking system.

In our war against the Infidels, we can't afford to stand divided.

That's why I've issued HR edict #439, Establishment of Lackadaisical Attitudes and Necessary Energy Release. It's a policy that encourages--and when we say "encourages" you know what we mean--each employee to be responsible for his own life energy and not waste it on petty office squabbles. The more energy we expend fighting each other, the less we have to fight the enemy. Plus, the edict spells out ELANER which I just think is a lovely name.

I know that some of you are less than thrilled by western science, but it offers some key insights into why the conservation of office energy principles works. Studies done at major universities show that when a group focuses its collective and determined hatred outward instead of inward, much more can be accomplished. That's really what we want for every member of this once-great Region: for you to live up to your potential and start culling the Infidel like we used to do. That's why they brought me in, and I think together we can do it!

So come on, team! Let's rally together and win one for the Big Guy, Allah!

Translated, retranslated memo: Praise Allah! Due to the sudden "relocation" of the HR Director, the position is now available.

MERRY CHRISTMAS SHOPPING?

Have you been shopping during the Christmas season lately? I don't mean online shopping in your pajamas, or perhaps a little less. I mean out and about, in the thick of it, wall to wall, terrible people assaulting you at every border kind of shopping. No? Well, you are missing out.

Last Christmas, I found myself in dire need of some extra presents. They were not the kind I could just order online unless I was comfortable signing over my only son as collateral to pay for shipping. Since practicality forced me into the jungles of commerce, planning was of the utmost importance. Once I knew the stores I needed to hit, I headed out into the madness.

Of course, being Washington State, it was raining. For some reason, Washingtonians don't know how to drive in the rain. I've lived here for more than 30 years and it still baffles me. Sensible things to do during a rainstorm are to slow down, drive cautiously, and do your best to see other vehicles through your ever-fogging windows. Alas, this never happens. Instead, Washington Drivers see the rain as a type of challenge, a YOLO call to action that inspires the most insane antics ever attempted with a car. People swerve in and out of lanes, cross through traffic, cutting everyone off, and test the limits of patience and wet brake pads. Seeing the mania all around me, I turned my wipers to high, cranked up the heat, and steeled myself for combat.

When Washington rain starts to come down in earnest, two personalities of driving quickly emerge. The first is the raving lunatic with nothing to live for, and a real wish to inflict a heart attack on some unsuspecting fellow driver. The second is the fellow driver susceptible to heart attacks by sudden movements and erratic behavior on the freeway. Then there are the unconverted, like myself, who get stuck behind the second type and feel themselves being transformed into the first. I mean, just go the speed limit, why is that so hard? And why are you stopping!? There's no one in front of you! It's just rain!

As I merged onto the freeway, a zippy white Passat, complete with chrome wheels and a trashy spoiler meant to convey "Yeah, I race," streaked by my passenger window. I watched as he navigated the shoulder into the merging traffic ahead, muffler loudly proclaiming his dominance in this battle, but causing all the other cars to grind to a halt. That's when I noticed the future heart attack victim in front of me and began to get nervous. He was slow to get started and, as the cars in front of him were getting up to speed to enter the freeway, he took his leisurely time. I looked behind me and saw an aggressively yellow race car surging forward, and it was like being an only child in the middle of mom and dad fighting.

At the first opportunity, the yellow car pulled onto the freeway behind me, splashing through a puddle and cutting off several cars, all to get two car lengths ahead. Of course, then he stopped and our lane passed him. I saw his fist slamming the air as we passed and I'm sure there were curses to follow. A part of me was pleased. That feeling of superiority was short-lived, as the Type 2 ahead of me refused to pick a comfortable speed on the freeway. I clenched the steering wheel, white-knuckled, and counted to ten.

I noticed, all too late, that the cars ahead of me were spraying water all over the road. It seemed a lake had formed in the right two lanes and the drivers hydroplaned through it with abandon. Before I knew what was happening, a torrent of water shot out from the tire of the car to my left and engulfed my windshield. I was driving blind at 50 miles per hour. As I reached to increase the speed of my windshield wipers, the thought struck me that anything could actually be in front of me at the moment and I wouldn't know. The Yeti, a brick wall, a pile of boulders, the lead singer for Nickelback, anything.

By the time I got to my first destination, the rain had eased up a little. The parking lot was barely occupied with only a few stray cars that I'm sure belonged to employees. I got out of the car and headed into the chocolate store to get a present for my Grandpa. I walked inside, grabbed my item and hopped in line. It struck me as odd that there was a line in the chocolate shop so early in the morning. I looked at my fellow linemates and saw that they also seemed to be buying presents and avoiding the Christmas rush. Only then did I notice that they were all looking at the counter.

The indecisive customer at the counter, taking up all the solitary employee's time, rocked back on his heels as stared at the chocolate case. He tapped his finger on his lips as if to draw out their secret desires for the next taste. This man was not shopping for gifts, he was clearly a man who indulged in morning chocolate. Which is worse, someone who buys early morning chocolates or early morning booze? Either way, it's a clear sign of a problem. He finally chose a dark chocolate, giving himself a self-satisfied grin, and we gift buyers were allowed to proceed through the line. One gift down.

My next to stop was to the bookstore, Barnes and Noble, to get my wife a book, which was foolish since they don't sell books at the bookstore anymore.

It was a surprise to me, as well. First, they took our other bookstores away and now they have changed the ones left into toy stores. My first view as I walked in was a wall of games, toys, and gaudy trinkets. No books. If you need a Round the World pencil holder or the latest copy of that kitschy kid's TV show they've somehow turned into a board game, however, you know where to go. Upon deeper inspection, I found that the store does indeed have books, just precious few of them. Try as I might, pingponging between their poorly laid out sections, I couldn't find the book I was looking for. So I made the brave decision to ask for help.

I got to the counter in time for a helpful associate, all twelve years and change on this earth, to render me some assistance. I gave her the title and author, and she set to work.

"We don't have that book in this store," she said.

"Yes, I know. I've looked." I told her.

"Oh, well," she punched in some numbers, "I could get it to you by New Years. Would that work?"

"No, I really need this as a Christmas present."

"Hmm, that could be a problem," she said as she clicked her fingernail on her teeth. Then her face brightened, "You could always write the title of the book down on a piece of paper and leave that as a gift." She said this with utmost seriousness and without any trace of irony.

"That's not going to happen," I told her plainly.

"You could always try online, maybe next-day shipping…" And that's where the conversation ended.

Someday, online stores will crack the same-day shipping code and we will all be rich and prosperous for it. And probably pantsless, since leaving the house will be a non-starter. But we will also lose stores like Barnes and Noble, where there's only room for thousands of books compared to the millions online I can search more easily. I gave up on B&N and left, empty handed. My whole plan was shot so I decided to double down on the misery and drive to the Tacoma Mall.

With all the cars rushing to buy love, I mean presents, the traffic was about as bad as you can imagine. A mile from the on-ramp, a white Lexus finally had enough of me driving responsibly, jerked into the next lane, rushed ahead, then cut me off. I assumed that it was because I don't feel the need to accelerate to the maximum in order to tailgate the person ahead of me. It's not my way.

Maybe we've always been poor drivers in the Northwest, but only recently have I begun to notice how bad. Not that I'm a great driver by any honest measure. I'm perhaps the first driver to admit this out loud. I've lost track of time while driving, spaced out, found myself going 20 in a 35 simply because I wasn't paying attention, only to be snapped out of my reverie by the honking behind me, weaving on the road because I'm convinced that I can grab that thing I dropped on the passenger floor and keep the car straight (spoiler: nope), and I've been that guy at the light who's fiddling with his radio when the light turns green sooner than he expected. I'll also admit that I'm a little afraid my insurance rate will go up now.

Instead of this making me a less patient person, all these mistakes have allowed me to have more grace for others, perhaps in the hopes that they would have grace for me. Alas, this doesn't seem to be the case. People always think they are the exceptions to the rule, especially while driving, and are more than willing to lay the blame at the other driver's stupidity or lack of brain cells. Don't get me wrong, some drivers really are idiots, but I'm getting to that.

When I finally got to the mall, I had to park 17 miles away and traverse a parking lot that had more in common with an ocean than a place to leave your car. Of course, I had left my umbrella in my wife's car. Hanging my coat over my head, my feet soaked through almost immediately, I dashed through the lot. There's a road in the middle of the lot, because, of course, and cars streaked through both ways with little regard for pedestrian life. There was no cross-walk. Seeing a break in the cars, I made my dash, feet splashing on the concrete. A truck in the far lane decided that this was the perfect time to speed up and it nearly hit me. I'm not sure if it was on purpose, but it did have a Trump bumper sticker, and several confederate flags, so perhaps he assumed I was homeless. Or an ISIS. Either way I obviously deserved whatever I had coming to me. I pirouetted around the truck as the driver honked. I'm not sure my ballet move did anything to move me up in his estimation. Cold, wet, and grumpy, but happy not to be a new hood ornament, I entered the temple of commerce known as Mall.

I don't like malls. Despite the roominess and space they offer, I always feel small and cramped. Maybe it's the fluorescent lit, overly fragrant, yet stale, air that makes me feel nauseous after only a few minutes. Or perhaps it's the onslaught of kiosk workers, assaulting me in broken English to test a product that obviously wasn't made for me (I'll pass on the makeup, thanks though). I headed directly to the Old Navy store where I know they have fleeces that my wife adores. The plan was to get in, get what I needed, then get out.

If my wife hadn't needed a fleece from their store, I would not have gone there. Old Navy has everything you need if you are into buying replacement clothes often.

I immediately felt out of place as the only man milling around in the women's department. Anytime I shop for my wife, I get those looks, the ones that say "you don't belong here," or "where is your escort?" I found some fleeces, but there were only a handful, all in colors she would hate, and sizes that she would find insulting in either direction.

I decided to do the sensible thing and find a store employee. After several minutes of searching, I finally noticed that Old Navy employees do not wear uniforms, or even a name tags, to make identification easier and stand out among the shoppers. I figure it's a way to avoid stupid questions like I was about to ask, but I'm a pro. I went to the dressing room. There was a 12-year-old stacking clothes on a rack, so I assumed that she was either an employee or the most helpful customer in the world. I apologized for bothering her, just in case she was a customer, and asked if she knew about the fleeces. She, of course, didn't, but radioed someone named Sherry with her half headset. Sherry answered and we walked briskly over to meet her at the fleeces.

With me properly disposed of, the dressing room attendant retreated to her cave. After hearing my story, Sherry was obviously not impressed with my gift choice, because she kept trying to direct me to other parts of the store. "Oh, you know what she would love..." she began, as if Sherry and my wife were old chums. I had to cut her off each time. When I convinced her I was firm about the fleece situation, she pursed her lips, nodded, and sighed. Then we walked over to the fleeces I had already found.

"These are the only ones I have," she confirms for me, "Here, what about this one?" She handed me a piece of clothing 2 sizes too big, in the almost-right color. Despite my desire not to have wasted a day shopping with nothing but peanut brittle to show for it, I know that buying something that had more in common with a tent than actual clothing would not endear me to my Love. I left, defeated once more, and walked out into the mall proper.

As people swirled around me, with happy looks of folks who had found what they needed, I had nothing. Why do people insist on wandering around stores physically when they can just go online and browse millions of instantly searchable shelves from home?

In fact, this is just what I did. I left the mall, drove home through rain and traffic, and decided not to press my luck with the mall any further. I ordered the presents online, informed my son he would have to work off our now incredible debt thanks to expedited shipping (he was upset, but understanding) and settled down into my recliner with a cold beer. It had been a long day.

THE MANLY CAMP
OF CHURCH MEN

Every year, my church hosts a man camp, a time away for men to engage in sport and activity while learning about the male-type creatures that God made us to be. It's not a retreat, but a time of testing and growth. It leaves you inspired, enlightened, and so sore that moving becomes a dreaded activity. My son and I attended and we couldn't have been more excited.

We arrived barely on time since the campground was near nowhere and just before the point of no return. We made our way down a winding road from the entrance, tall pines laying shadows in the failing evening sun. The final twist of the road revealed a cafeteria, outside of which several men sported beards many orders more wonderful than my genes allow. They were flexing arms and voices, psyching up for a weekend filled with scripture, male bonding, and bodily torture. Our pastor, Bo, was leading the throng. He nodded his head at us, seemingly in slow motion, as if he knew our deepest fears and they were now his to command. My excitement dimmed a bit.

We parked in the back lot and piled into the gym with all of the other men for the kick-off to the festivities. Once gathered, we received a brief introduction to the weekend and split into teams. Teams split into ordinary colors like blue, orange green, but then branched off into unnecessarily complicated ones like rainbow, paisley, and maize. I felt deeply for the pink team, though, to their credit, they kept their spirits and masculinity firmly intact. One of the teams had an abundance of ex-military and West Point grads, or so I was told. I couldn't help but think that they had a slight advantage in the trials and tasks ahead.

Dinner was served in the cafeteria buffet-style. After getting up and standing in line, I found out too late that I had entered the salad line instead of the real food line. My son was obviously disappointed until I revealed my plan all along, which I made up on the spot: to get salad so we had something to eat while we waited in the line for real food. He thought I was a genius. Score. He's almost 17 and rarely gets the chance to think of his dad as brilliant.

Dinner eaten, our next activities were in the chapel up the hill. Entering the chapel, the strong odor of musty, mildew-covered mold, probably toxic, but nostalgic nonetheless, overpowered my sense of smell. We all sat down and began a game. I was told there would be silly games, but our first involved a straw, two plates, and M&M's. The goal was to move the candy from one plate to the other using the sucking power of your mouth. The cheers of "Suck, Suck, Suck" were probably the first of their kind ever heard in that sacred place. The phrase "You sucked" actually became a compliment. My son was chosen to suck for our team, and he sucked admirably, though the winning team was Pink, which I thought was wonderful. We worshiped together and learned from the Word, how to take Kingship over our lives and act like men. It was great lesson and set the tone for the weekend, as Bo told us that we better "man up" because boyhood was quickly coming to an end. We would soon be playing dodgeball.

For those that don't know, dodgeball is a game where men, though usually boys, and sometimes women (though not often because they have more sense about these things) throw rubber balls at each other in an attempt to kill or maim. That's how it seems at least. If you are unfortunate enough to get hit with a ball, you must leave the court immediately (or sometimes not at all, depending on your willingness to cheat), and the team with the most players standing at the end wins. There are other rules--something about dropping balls and going out of bounds--but they were safely ignored by all players without penalty.

Our team, christened the "Manroons," thanks to our maroon headbands and excessively manly natures (plus, it's just plain fun to bellow), held our own and reached the semi-finals. This was not due to any help I provided. I've never liked dodgeball and usually shy away from any overly-aggressive games, so I was looking for a way to redeem myself. The chance came with the tie breaker that would send our team into the finals (against a military juggernaut of destruction). We would be shooting free throws to determine which team would go to the finals, and which would play the loser's bracket. This was something I thought I could do, having played basketball before. I also felt I owed my team something since I spent a large portion of our dodgeball matches either praying that I wouldn't get hit, or just thankful when I did because that meant I could cheer from the sidelines. Finally, I could contribute meaningfully to the team.

I stepped up to the line, bounced the ball twice in front of my feet, as was my routine many years before, spun the ball in my right hand, brought it up to the top of my head, and propelled it toward the rim, making sure to add in some follow through. Follow through is where you snap your wrist at the end of your shot to add spin to the ball. I'm sure there's a complicated reason for doing this, relating to physics and such, but I wasn't thinking about any of that as I put a lovely spin on the ball. It sailed through the air, straight and true, perfectly in line with the rim. It just never got to the rim. The ball didn't even touch the net.

This is called an air ball and is about the most embarrassing thing a man can do at man camp, or in life. There are a few exceptions; laughing at a funeral, developing an obsession with My Little Pony (called Bronies, look it up), but air balls when victory is on the line is definitely up there. I tried to regroup as I was passed the ball, but my confidence was bruised. I tried not to look at my teammates. I tried to focus. I bounced, I spun, I launched.

I shot yet another air ball.

This was bad--like my teammates, and even other teams, coming up to pat me on the back in commis-erating support bad. You want cheers, not supportive pats on the back. But when you're shooting airballs, I suppose you take what you can get. I still had one more shot, and I tried my best block everything else out.

I bounced.

I spun.

I hoisted and shot.

This one felt like it had more momentum than the others, and it was right down the middle. It didn't airball (yay!) but it did strike the back of the rim so hard that a powerful thud reverberated from the rim, into the wall, and shook the entire gym, rattling our shoes. I was 0 for 3. Now I know how Charlie Brown felt. My free throw opponent had only to make one out of three to win, and their victory seemed all but certain.

But then he missed his first two shots and my heart leaped just a little. If he didn't make any shots either, we would get to shoot again and I would get my chance at redemption.

He shot his last ball, a lazy floater that bounced twice, then rolled around the rim as if it was looking for lost keys, before falling in and sealing our fate. We went on to take 4th place, but lost the opportunity to take 1st, which will always haunt me. I don't like competition, but I'm competitive, go figure. (In case you're wondering, the Starship Troopers won).

After the scheduled activities, a few of us hung around the gym to play some basketball. I was reminded, not for the last time, that I'm not as young as I hoped. However, the camaraderie and late night conversations more than made up for any aches and pains that wracked my out-of-shape body.

The next morning, I woke up with the type of hangover you get when you stay up much too late. Only older people understand this. I skipped a cold shower in favor of coffee, which seemed a reasonable trade in my groggy state. Over coffee and hot chocolate, Sean and I had a wonderful talk about how the message from the night before applied to our lives. It was one of those great father-son moments.

On our way to the morning gathering in the gym, we walked past an eight-foot tall wooden bear that we hadn't seen the night before. The craftsmanship was excellent and we could tell it was lovingly made. There was just one problem. The bear had one arm crossing his body in suspiciously coy manner while making a Nazi salute with the other. Strangely, no one else seemed bothered by Coy, Hail Hitler Bear but I was determined to get to the bottom of the matter.

We all gathered for prayer and encouragement in the gym. After we finished, one of the camp leaders mentioned that bacon would be served at breakfast and everyone's spirits rose. Bo seemed especially happy. We shuffled into the dining hall for our morning feast and when everyone was seated, a camp staffer bravely announced that each person would be limited to 3 pieces of bacon. Total. The mood changed. The air hummed with tension and I heard several growls around the tables. The staffer slowly backed away, making sure to keep his eyes forward and hands out as if to pacify the tired, now angry men. To his credit, he delivered the harsh news with courage, knowing that his announcement could potentially cause a riot. Thankfully, there was enough bacon to go around and the men kept their cool.

I went up to the staffer after breakfast and complimented him on his composure. I also asked about the Coy Hitler Bear. He assured me that there were no Nazi sympathizers among the camp, but rather, the statue was a gift to the camp from a foreman who had helped with a recent remodel. Apparently, he carved wooden bears in his off-hours and had one to spare. They called it the Potty Bear because he looked like he was raising his hand up, as if asking permission to use the bathroom while holding his bladder. I admitted that this interpretation was far more charitable than my own, but he couldn't tell me exactly what the bear meant.

But Coy Nazi Bears were not the camp's only oddities. Just outside the front doors of the cafeteria is a building called "The Old Pumphouse Espresso." Old Pumphouse conjures images of jaunty swill being dumped into a waiting cup, not finely crafted European drinks. I dare you to find a less appealing name for a coffee joint. And no, Starbucks doesn't count.

After breakfast, we poured into the musty chapel for more teaching and I was struck by a cross outside the window. It was a simple cross, just some logs slung together, but it made me think of how odd Christians are compared to everyone else. We glorify our leader's instrument of torture and death, raising it up as the ultimate symbol of victory. I know I'm not the first, or last, Christian to make this observation, but it struck me as significant.

After the chapel session, we trudged outside and gathered in a cold, muddy field. My fellow Manroons attempted to frighten me with tales of the previous year's competition, something to do with lifting massive logs and moving them down a field, nearly killing each other, then having to chop them into tiny pieces. I didn't see any logs, which I took as a positive sign, but my veteran teammates feared the worst. I told them it couldn't be that bad. We were all wrong. Instead of afflicting our bodies, the Man Camp organizers came for our minds instead.

It was a relay race of epic proportions. We began, as so many do, with the three-legged race and proceeded through a series of increasingly heinous challenges. After the 3-legged race, we had to drink an entire two-liter of extra fizzy seltzer from a bowl using just straws. It perhaps wasn't extra fizzy on purpose, but my quickly assaulted nostrils didn't know the difference. Once we had slurped the last bit of seltzer from the bowl, one teammate ran to the opposite end of the field and came back with three bags of random food.

The mental fortitude you must summon to drink

lots of seltzer water is nothing compared to consuming an entire stick of unsalted butter, which is what one of our brave teammates was tasked to do. If you've never shoved an entire handful of Crisco in your mouth, you have no idea how tough you must be to eat a stick of plain butter. Our comrade's steely gaze intensified with every bite of the hated golden block. While I know that it all went down, that was not the butter's final resting place, as much of it vaulted up to torment him again. With the last bite, and a look of pained triumph, he raised his arms in victory. Our next challenges of building a lego house from memory, building a fire to free a golf ball from a block of ice, then tossing that golf ball into a five-gallon bucket (golf balls bounce, a lot), paled in comparison to the food. It was an epic force of will. Other teams had to eat a green pepper, peaches, or some grapefruit, but they know nothing of pain, heartache, and that nasty coating on the inside of your mouth. Our team managed second, but in courage, strong will, and dedication we were winners. I'll give you one guess for which team won, again.

For lunch, we were treated to burgers and an extra hour of free time, then it was off to the next challenge.

During the final physical challenge, I discovered that if I was a human foosball player, I would be awkward and terrible at it. My foot-eye coordination was perhaps worse than my hand-eye coordination during dodgeball. After human foosball, we played a bean-bag tossing game just to prove to everyone that I'm not a gifted athlete. I worried that my complete lack of athletic ability would turn my teammates against me. Thankfully, men in my church are vicious on the battlefield, but forgiving in equal measure, taking joy in the heat of combat while wholeheartedly comforting their fellow man in trouble.

Our final event was trivia and the stakes couldn't have been higher. The Manroons were trailing but within striking distance of victory. I felt the distinct possibility of redeeming myself.

We began answering questions and it was obvious that there was no need for me to redeem myself. It wasn't about me or my pride. We worked as a team. I finally began to realize that it wasn't about performing well as an individual, it was more important to win together.

The final question, styled like final Jeopardy, was about sports. Since none of the Manroons were all that confident in the subject, we bet only the points that we felt comfortable losing. As luck would have it, we knew the answer, but fortune favored the bold. The teams who went all in came out on top and we ended up with the bronze.

In the end, I learned that it's not about who is better. The team that dominated other categories didn't do well in the trivia. My unfounded bitterness was completely my own. It's the effort that matters, not the results, and I had lost sight of that. Thankfully, we were all gracious to each other, and learned how to be good winners and otherwise.

I can't wait for next year.

ACKNOWLEDGEMENTS

Thank you to my wife, who puts up with my nonsense and lets me know when I'm being less than charitable, but also encourages my funny side. I wouldn't have written this book without her support. Also to my son who still laughs at my jokes and serves as my guinea pig, whether he knows it or not.

Lots of folks contributed to these stories, wittingly and otherwise. Robert Root, my friend, who shared his sense of humor with me and gave me some great feedback. Mike Leamer for allowing me to write about our little trip and making me laugh the entire time. Much thanks to Bill Bryson, whose comedic stylings inspired me to see the world a little differently and write a few stories of my own.

Also, a big thanks to my editor, Jenelle Ashmore, who made sure my books made sense and removed all the mistakes. My work reads much better because of your tireless effort.

More Titles from Josh Kilen

The Tales of Big and Little
Doom of the Three Stones
Shirlee's Revenge
The End of the Worlds

The Lost Princess Series
The Lost Princess in Winter's Grip
The Lost Princess in The Shifting Sands
The Lost Princess in Destiny's Call

The Adventures of Sean Ryanis
Sean Ryanis & The Impossible Chase
Sean Ryanis & The Brink of Oblivion

The Superhero Chronicles
Birth of Moonlight

Non-Fiction Titles
Walking the Narrow Road: Instruction for Christians In Business
Social Joy: Marketing for Artists
Choreawseome!
Go Write Now
Killer Deals

Electing to Win

Also, Books For Kids Inspired by MINECRAFT

Rise of the Master Creeper Saga
Golem Battle
Master of the Creepers
The Master's Last Stand

The Glitch Battle Series
The Lair of Doom
The Portal to the Nether
Down With the Glitch

Steve and Dr. Jakesh Series
Mutant Spiders of Destruction
More coming soon!

Steve and the Curator Series
The Terror of Angels
More coming soon!

Just visit Joshkilen.com to find more books you are sure to love!

You're still here?

It's over!

Go home.

Go.

Made in the
USA
Monee, IL